Feasting on the Word®

ADVENT COMPANION

Feasting on the Word®
ADVENT COMPANION

A THEMATIC RESOURCE
FOR PREACHING AND WORSHIP

EDITED BY

David L. Bartlett
Barbara Brown Taylor
Kimberly Bracken Long

COMPILED BY

Jessica Miller Kelley

WJK WESTMINSTER
JOHN KNOX PRESS
LOUISVILLE · KENTUCKY

First edition
Published by Westminster John Knox Press
Louisville, Kentucky

14 15 16 17 18 19 20 21 22 23—10 9 8 7 6 5 4 3 2 1

Book design by Drew Stevens
Cover design by Lisa Buckley and Dilu Nicholas

Library of Congress Cataloging-in-Publication Data

Feasting on the Word Advent companion : a thematic resource for
preaching and worship / compiled by Jessica Miller Kelley ; edited by
David L. Bartlett, Barbara Brown Taylor, and Kimberly Bracken Long.
  pages cm
 ISBN 978-0-664-25964-8 (alk. paper)
 1. Advent. 2. Worship programs. 3. Common lectionary (1992)
 I. Kelley, Jessica Miller, compiler.
 BV40.F43 2014
 263'.912—dc23

                                                    2014008811

Contents

Introduction

Advent comes every year, with the same challenges for church leaders everywhere. While it is the beginning of a new liturgical and lectionary year, the approach of the calendar year's end looms with pressure for church budgets and record keeping, not to mention the crush of holiday to-dos and travel plans making the presence and participation of members and staff alike a bit spotty.

Telling the incarnation story afresh each year to busy and distracted people is perhaps one of the greatest challenges for pastors this season, even more so because this may be the one time of the year when disaffected and dechurched people decide to give church another try. The high calling to edify lifelong disciples while engaging those on the margins of the church demands continual reconsideration of the stories and themes that form the foundation of our Christian faith.

Feasting on the Word Advent Companion is designed for those who do not follow the lectionary during Advent, or those lectionary preachers who want a different option during Advent. It offers an alternative and supplement to the Revised Common Lectionary for the Sundays of Advent as well as Christmas Eve and Christmas Day. This resource suggests an Old Testament and Gospel passage for each service, presenting opportunities to explore traditional Advent themes through prophetic announcements of the Lord's coming, the narratives surrounding Christ's birth, and Jesus' own declarations about the Day of the Lord still to come. These texts were chosen from Old Testament and Gospel passages that are frequently preached from during the Advent season. The resources in this *Companion* are a combination of material from existing *Feasting on the Word* volumes as well as newly written material.

In keeping with other *Feasting on the Word* resources, the *Advent Companion* offers pastors focused resources for sermon preparation along with ready-to-use liturgies for a complete order of worship. Four essays provide theological, pastoral, exegetical, and homiletical perspectives on each of the day's two texts. These essays are written by scholars, pastors, seminary professors, and denominational leaders, offering a bounty of starting points for the preacher to consider. Hymn suggestions are included to support each day's scriptural and theological focus. Optional prayers for use during the Eucharist are provided in the back of the book. In addition, a children's sermon is included for each service, making the themes and texts of Advent accessible to all ages in the congregation. These stories will enrich their experience of worship while respecting both a child's intelligence and theological integrity.

To expand and enhance the congregation's experience of Advent, midweek services are also provided in this volume. These abbreviated liturgies and sample homilies are ideal for use in an existing morning or midday worship offering, Wednesday night programming, or a special series offered just for the weeks of Advent. These resources may also offer additional inspiration for planning Sunday worship. Finally, a service of healing, often called a Longest Night service, is provided for the many churches who hold such a service during the Christmas season.

As Christmas's cultural and commercial value increases evermore, the spiritual grounding of Advent expectation becomes more and more essential. Taking time for personal reflection and family devotion becomes just another item on parishioners' long to-do lists, often falling below endless shopping, wrapping, baking, and hosting. Sunday worship and Christmas Eve services are their primary opportunities to stop and consider the timeless truth and lasting promise of Advent, and pastors' primary opportunity to touch hearts and lives during this special season.

Overview of Advent

A dvent, which marks the beginning of a new church year, begins four Sundays prior to Christmas Day. It can be as long as twenty-eight days, if December 25 falls on a Sunday, or as short as twenty-two days, if December 25 falls on a Monday, making Christmas Eve the fourth Sunday of Advent.

During the Advent season, the church prepares for the coming of Christ. Even as we make ready for the baby to be born in Bethlehem, the themes and texts explored during Advent take us beyond the birth, and even beyond the life, death, and resurrection of Jesus, to a new moment of expectancy as the Day of Christ approaches and the reign of God is made fully manifest.

People who "faint from fear and foreboding" (Luke 21:26) intrude on our sanitized image of the manger scene in Luke 2, revealing the complexity of Advent's scope. It may seem strange and uncomfortable for some in the congregation to begin Advent with weeping and laments, but it is a discomfort with meaning. It is where we need to begin. The coming of Advent jolts the church out of Ordinary Time with the invasive news that it is time to think about fresh possibilities for deliverance and human wholeness. Peace is at the heart of the promise born at Advent, but it is difficult to arrive there safely and without becoming vulnerable along the way. It is difficult to set out on the journey without repentance and forgiveness.

At Advent, God's people summon the courage and the spiritual strength to remember that the holy breaks into the daily. In tiny ways, we can open our broken hearts to the healing grace of God, who opens the way to peace. May that peace come upon us as a healing balm, as a mighty winter river, gushing and rushing through the valleys of our prideful fear and our own self-righteous indignation. Advent is not a season for passive waiting and watching. It is a season of wailing and weeping, of opening up our lives and our souls with active anticipation and renewed hope.

Weekly Texts and Themes

	Old Testament	Gospel	Theme
First Sunday of Advent	Jeremiah 33:14–16	Luke 21:5–19	Hope, expectation, preparation
Second Sunday of Advent	Malachi 3:1–4	Matt. 24:36–44	Purification, righteousness, fulfillment
Third Sunday of Advent	Zephaniah 3:14–20	Mark 13:24–37	Love, peace, the presence of the Lord
Fourth Sunday of Advent	Psalm 146:5–10	Luke 1:46b–55	Justice, joy, salvation
Christmas Eve	Isaiah 9:2–7	Luke 2:1–14 (15–20)	The promise fulfilled, God with us
Christmas Day	Isaiah 52:7–10	John 1:1–14	New creation, light of the world

Texts for Midweek Services

	Old Testament	Gospel	Theme
Week One	Isaiah 57:14–19	Luke 1:5–25 (optional, vv. 57–80)	John prepares the way as a new prophet, turning hearts to God
Week Two	Isaiah 40:1–11	Mark 1:1–8	John preaches repentance in advance of Christ's coming
Week Three	Isaiah 11:1–10	John 1:29–34	John proclaims Jesus as the Messiah long promised
Week Four	Isaiah 35:1–10	Matthew 11:2–11	John lets Jesus take center stage

First Sunday of Advent

Jeremiah 33:14–16

¹⁴The days are surely coming, says the LORD, when I will fulfill the promise I made to the house of Israel and the house of Judah. ¹⁵In those days and at that time I will cause a righteous Branch to spring up for David; and he shall execute justice and righteousness in the land. ¹⁶In those days Judah will be saved and Jerusalem will live in safety. And this is the name by which it will be called: "The LORD is our righteousness."

Luke 21:5–19

⁵When some were speaking about the temple, how it was adorned with beautiful stones and gifts dedicated to God, he said, ⁶"As for these things that you see, the days will come when not one stone will be left upon another; all will be thrown down."

⁷They asked him, "Teacher, when will this be, and what will be the sign that this is about to take place?" ⁸And he said, "Beware that you are not led astray; for many will come in my name and say, 'I am he!' and, 'The time is near!' Do not go after them.

⁹"When you hear of wars and insurrections, do not be terrified; for these things must take place first, but the end will not follow immediately." ¹⁰Then he said to them, "Nation will rise against nation, and kingdom against kingdom; ¹¹there will be great earthquakes, and in various places famines and plagues; and there will be dreadful portents and great signs from heaven.

¹²"But before all this occurs, they will arrest you and persecute you; they will hand you over to synagogues and prisons, and you will be brought before kings and governors because of my name. ¹³This will give you an opportunity to testify. ¹⁴So make up your minds not to prepare your defense in advance; ¹⁵for I will give you words and a wisdom that none of your opponents will be able to withstand or contradict. ¹⁶You will be betrayed even by parents and brothers, by relatives and friends; and they will put some of you to death. ¹⁷You will be hated by all because of my name. ¹⁸But not a hair of your head will perish. ¹⁹By your endurance you will gain your souls."

ORDER OF WORSHIP

OPENING WORDS / CALL TO WORSHIP
> The days are surely coming, says the Lord,   *Jer. 33:14–16*
> when I will fulfill my promise to my people.
> **Justice and righteousness will fill the land**
> **and all will live in peace and safety.**

LIGHTING OF THE ADVENT CANDLES
> *[Reader 1]:* We light this candle as a symbol
>   of the hope we have in the promise of the
>   Lord's coming.
> *[Reader 2]:* For the Lord will fulfill his promise
>   to the house of Israel and the house of Judah.
>   A righteous Branch will spring up for David;
>   and he shall execute justice and righteousness
>   in the land.
> *[All]:* **Come, Lord Jesus, come!**

HYMN, SPIRITUAL, OR PSALM

CALL TO CONFESSION
> Testify with honesty the condition of your souls.   *Luke 21:13–14*
> Give defense not for yourself but only the
>   Lord's grace,
> which will save you in your time of trial.
> With confidence in God's mercy,
> let us confess our sin.

PRAYER OF CONFESSION
> **Lord, have mercy on us.**
> **We are not ready for your coming.**
> **We live in sin, as though there were no justice.**
> **We live in fear, as though there were no grace.**
> **Forgive us, Lord.**
> **Show us your mercy and steadfast love.**
> **Lead us in your truth, and teach us your paths,**
> **for you are the God of our salvation. Amen.**

DECLARATION OF FORGIVENESS

The Lord is our righteousness. *Jer. 33:16*
In Christ, we are forgiven.

PRAYER OF THE DAY

Holy One, you have promised us
that the day of our salvation is near.
Keep us faithful in love and watchful in prayer,
so that we may stand with confidence and joy
at the coming of Christ, our redeemer and Lord. **Amen.**

HYMN, SPIRITUAL, OR PSALM

PRAYER FOR ILLUMINATION

Amid much confusion,
signs leading away from you,
we seek your truth.
Open our hearts *Luke 21:15*
to the wonders of your work
and the wisdom of your word. **Amen.**

SCRIPTURE READINGS

SERMON

HYMN, SPIRITUAL, OR PSALM

PRAYERS OF INTERCESSION

[A brief silence may follow each petition.]
Let us pray to the Lord, saying,
in your mercy, Lord, save us.

Merciful God,
you call us to goodness and lead us on right paths.
You encourage us with signs of your coming
and urge us to keep watch,
that we might greet you with heads raised high
when you come to restore all of creation.
Watching and waiting, we pray for this world that
needs your saving power.

For nations at war,
    in your mercy, **Lord, save us.**
For all who suffer from violence, in the streets or in their homes,
    in your mercy, **Lord, save us.**
For all who live in worry or fear,
    in your mercy, **Lord, save us.**
For those who have forgotten the ways of righteousness,
    in your mercy, **Lord, save us.**
For those who have never heard of your rescuing love,
    in your mercy, **Lord, save us.**
For all those who have lost hope, or never had it at all,
    in your mercy, **Lord, save us.**

We pray, too, for your church in the world,
that we may increase in ardor for you and your children,
and work in confidence for your coming reign.
Now by the power of your Holy Spirit, make us ever more faithful,
that we may greet you in confidence and joy on that great day;
    through Christ, in whose name we pray. **Amen.**

LORD'S PRAYER

INVITATION TO THE OFFERING
Trusting in the sure promises of Christ,
and grateful for the Spirit's sustaining power,
let us bring our tithes and offerings to God.

PRAYER OF THANKSGIVING/DEDICATION
God of righteousness,
you have saved us from the worst the world can do
and have promised to redeem the whole creation when
    Christ comes again.
In faith and hope we offer our gifts of money and self,
that we may be part of what you are doing in the world even now,
as we watch for Christ's coming in glory. **Amen.**

HYMN, SPIRITUAL, OR PSALM

CHARGE
Hear with your hearts   *Luke 21:15*
the word and wisdom of the Lord.

May the God of mercy keep you,
the Holy Spirit cheer you,
and Christ in glory greet you,
now and at the day of his coming.

SONG SUGGESTIONS

Included are songbook numbers for *Chalice Hymnal* (*CH*), the Episcopal Church's *Hymnal 1982* (*EH*), *Evangelical Lutheran Worship* (*ELW*), *Gather Comprehensive*, 2nd ed. (*GC*), *Glory to God: The Presbyterian Hymnal* (*GTG*), *The New Century Hymnal* (*TNCH*), and the *United Methodist Hymnal* (*UMH*).

"Come, Thou Long-Expected Jesus" (*CH* 125, *EH* 66, *ELW* 254, *GC* 323, *GTG* 82–83, *TNCH* 122, *UMH* 196)
"Comfort, Comfort Now My People" (*CH* 122–123, *EH* 67, *ELW* 256, *GC* 326, *GTG* 87, *TNCH* 101)
"Light One Candle to Watch for Messiah," stanza 1 (*ELW* 240, *GTG* 85)
"O Come, O Come, Emmanuel" (*CH* 119, *ELW* 257, *GC* 317, *GTG* 88, *TNCH* 116, *UMH* 211)
"O Day of God, Draw Nigh" (*TNCH* 611, *UMH* 730)
"The Days Are Surely Coming" (*GTG* 357)
"To a Maid Whose Name Was Mary" (*GTG* 98, *UMH* 215)
"While We Are Waiting, Come" (*GTG* 92)

CHILDREN'S SERMON

Based on Jeremiah 33:14–16, with references to Isaiah 43 and Malachi 4:5–6

Things look different in church this time of year. We use blue or purple cloth and candles, and we have evergreen wreaths and garland. This time of year, when we start getting ready to celebrate Jesus' birth at Christmas, is called Advent. Advent is a time of expectation. "Expectation" means "looking forward to something," and during Advent, we are looking forward to Jesus being born. During Advent, we read about the things that happened before Jesus was born and imagine what it would have been like to be living before Jesus was born, looking forward to when he would come.

God's people in Judah a long, long time ago had a lot of scary things happen to them. Armies and kings from other countries invaded their land and took over. The people were scared, but God promised to send a savior to rescue them. God gave people called "prophets" messages to give the people hope. The prophets said, "Do not give up hope. A savior is coming. God promised, and God does not break promises."

The prophets used stories the people already knew, to help them watch for the savior. They said that when the savior comes, it would be like the great king David was still on the throne, back when you were safe and no armies and kings from other countries were taking over. It would be like when Moses parted the sea to lead the people out of slavery in Egypt, into the promised land. It would be like that very special prophet, Elijah, coming back to make our people righteous again.

The people knew about David and Moses and Elijah. David and Moses and Elijah were heroes to these people, so they knew that if the savior would be like these heroes—or even better than them—this savior must be really, really special. So they kept watching and hoping for when God would send the savior.

Even though we live a long time after Jesus, we still watch and hope for him, because he really is a very, very special savior.

Prayer: Thank you, God, for sending Jesus to us. Amen.

SERMON HELPS

Jeremiah 33:14–16

THEOLOGICAL PERSPECTIVE

This brief essay will attend to the continuing theological significance of (1) the reality of human despair, (2) a reading of the promise in light of both the experience of exile and the practice of waiting in Advent, and (3) the collective and sociopolitical aspects of the promise.

The Reality of Human Despair. Much of the story told in Jeremiah has to do with the threat and fulfillment of the destruction of Judah and, in particular, Jerusalem. The people have been violating their covenantal relationship with God, and the subsequent Babylonian control would serve as punishment for their infidelity. The complete sacking of Jerusalem, however, is more horrific and absolute than the people might have imagined. The destruction is so severe that God's voice, through the prophet, also wails in lamentation.

In view of the devastation that characterizes the sociohistorical context of the "Book of Consolation," Kathleen O'Connor describes the situation of the people in this way: "The people... are taken captive, dragged from their land, and deprived of their Temple. They are beaten, imprisoned, and face death as a people, and, like Jeremiah, they cry out to God in anger and despair."[1] John Calvin imagined the context in even more explicit terms: "As they were then exposed to slaughter, . . . the children of God saw thousand deaths; so that it could not be but that terror almost drove them to despair; and in their exile they saw that they were far removed from their own country, without any hope of a return."[2]

When faced with such death, slaughter, and imprisonment in a strange place, who would not despair? While despair is among the most human of human conditions, it cannot be fully understood apart from its theological implications. In a number of his writings, Reinhold Niebuhr associated despair with our failed attempts to procure security for ourselves, optimistically pretending that we are not subject to the vicissitudes of creatureliness. Despair is characterized primarily by the conspicuous absence of theological hope. Humans meet despair when they cannot imagine God's promised alternative future.

God's Promise to a People Waiting. The writer recounts the promises made to "the house of Israel and the house of Judah," that God would provide the people a safe, just, and peaceful future under a justly appointed and righteous ruler. This week's reading is addressed to a people in exile. God's promise, in this case, is meant to be a comfort and source of hope to the exiled, rather than a foretelling of the faithful remnant that appears between Jeremiah's condemnations of unjust rulers. Here we meet the God who promises to protect and restore the people, even as they are in the midst of great suffering and at the edge of despair. It is in precisely this context that God speaks the promise, and it is in precisely this context that despair opens the door to creativity and hope. Calvin acknowledged that the promises of God seem to disappear, but that with faith and patience, we look forward to their fulfillment.

In part, this is the theological significance of Advent too. The inclusion of prophetic literature in the Advent lections points to the importance of

---

1. Kathleen O'Connor, "Jeremiah," in *The Women's Bible Commentary*, ed. Carol A. Newsom and Sharon H. Ringe (Louisville, KY: Westminster John Knox Press, 2002), 174.
2. John Calvin, *Commentaries on the Book of the Prophet Jeremiah and the Lamentations*, vol. 4, ed. and trans. John Owen (Grand Rapids: Eerdmans, 1950), 247. http://www.ccel.org/ccel/calvin/calcom20.i.html (accessed from Christian Classics Ethereal Library).

waiting, anticipating, and trusting in a promised future that seems very removed from our current circumstance. And it is in the season of Advent that we engage in the strenuous and crucial Christian task of *imagination.* Together with the prophet, we are called not only to name suffering and injustice, but to lean into God's promised alternative future.

Theological imagination is not speculative, but relies on God's continuous presence and acts on behalf of creation over time. Trusting in God's provision for us in the past, we imagine what shape God's fulfillment of promises will take in the future. Although we do not bring about God's intended alternative future through sheer force of will, in our waiting we do try to place ourselves in a posture so that we might become partners with God in the advent of a new reality.

The Collective and Sociopolitical Aspects of God's Promise. The promise Jeremiah recalls is not an otherworldly, escapist spirituality that encourages us merely to "wait it out." Particularly in the prophetic literature, and echoed in Gospel texts like the Magnificat (Luke 1:46–55), we find repeated affirmations that God's promise includes a transvaluation of social, economic, and political relationships. In this particular lection, the prophet anticipates a time in which even the failed leadership will be made aright and "do what kings are supposed to do, namely, practice justice and righteousness. . . . When the king practices justice and righteousness, the city and the land will be healed and saved."[3] In the creative moment of near-despair, the prophet calls us to imagine a new social context in which we live together in safety, peace, and righteousness. God will do this, as promised, and even bring about new life for the city.

JENNIFER RYAN AYRES

PASTORAL PERSPECTIVE

"In those days . . ." On Christmas Eve Luke will turn the church back to a historical context of Jesus' birth, anchoring the event in time with persons and places, in a world of Caesar and census: "In those days a decree went out from Emperor Augustus that all the world should be registered" (Luke 2:1). But on the First Sunday of Advent, Jeremiah turns us forward to the future: "In those days and at that time . . ." In these days before Christmas the future is not where our culture encourages us to go; it fosters a holiday experience that is nostalgic and immediate. "In those days and at that time" God will

---

3. Walter Brueggemann, *A Commentary on Jeremiah: Exile and Homecoming,* 2nd ed. (Grand Rapids: Eerdmans, 1998), 318.

decree justice and righteousness. Seasonal traditions dictate charity. "The days are surely coming" when God will fulfill the promise. We are sure that consumerism will deliver our fulfillment. The church is called to hear the prophets in this season, not for "once upon a time" background music, but for an overture playing in real time, sounding themes to be developed going forward. "In those days" there will be "justice and righteousness," peace and security. The church may light its Advent candles for preparation, hope, joy, and love, but the prophets sound justice and righteousness.

A pastoral perspective on Advent is attuned to the yearnings of our day for a different day, and aware of both the temptation to look backward for God and good and the trepidation in looking forward. The prophet Jeremiah speaks a pastoral word, assuring the people of his time and ours that what is coming is of God. He is adamant about the things that we are tentative about: "The days are surely coming . . ." (here and in 23:5–6; see also 31:27, 31, 38); "I have . . . plans for your welfare and not for harm, to give you a future with hope" (29:11). There will be a future in God's time and fulfillment on God's terms. This particular text envisions not a day to come at Advent's end, but days to come that will inaugurate a new beginning.

The congregation that observes Advent will mark time differently from those people who live December as a countdown to Christmas and the end of the year. The Sundays of Advent count forward to a time that begins with the birth of Christ. The First Sunday of Advent is for Christians the first Sunday of the year, a new year in sacred time, opening to the mystery and certainty of God's presence. Worship that celebrates an alternative New Year's Day affirms time as God's home and workplace, not as a calendar of accumulating years but as a movement toward fulfillment, not a day for self-improvement resolutions but for community reaffirmation of trust in God's promises, past, present, and future. "With grateful hearts the past we own; The future, all to us unknown, We to your guardian care commit." Philip Doddridge wrote on the manuscript of his hymn, "For the New Year."[4]

Jeremiah 33:14–16 preached on the First Sunday in Advent rightly leads to the Eucharist; in this sacrament believers are nourished by the hope of God's coming and participate in God's future. An Advent liturgy recalls that through the words of the prophets God promised the Redeemer, "and gave hope for the day when justice shall roll down like waters, and righteousness like an ever rolling stream."[5] Prayers that are evoked by this text will acknowledge God as the One who lives and moves and comes to us in time

4. Philip Doddridge (1702–51), "Great God, We Sing That Mighty Hand," in *The Presbyterian Hymnal* (Louisville, KY: Westminster/John Knox Press, 1990), 265.
5. *The Book of Common Worship* (Louisville, KY: Westminster/John Knox Press, 1993), 133.

and who works justice and righteousness in all times; they will express gratitude for time as God's good gift; they will confess our preoccupation with the immediate and our fear of the future; they will ask for our confidence in God's tomorrow and pray for those who yearn for the justice and righteousness that they will not know in their days.

Congregational life during Advent that is faithful to the prophetic vision of "the days . . . surely coming" emphasizes political as well as personal relationships. This text insists that covenantal life in all its expressions is characterized by justice and righteousness, allowing no dichotomy of "prophetic" and "pastoral." Life together is to embody the nature of God, "The Lord is our righteousness." Jeremiah uses the name first for a promised person (23:6) and again here, intentionally, for a promised place (33:16). The vision of the time to come impugns the time at hand. What leader and what community could claim "The Lord is our righteousness"? The promise challenges our reality, and drives a reappropriation of "righteousness." The word is uncommon, if not pejorative, in common parlance and unwelcome in the lexicon of many faithful because of its frequent companionship with "self."

One of the pastoral tasks is to teach the vocabulary of faith, and "righteousness" is one of the first words of the language of Advent. In Matthew's Gospel, "righteousness" is Jesus' first word, spoken to John the Baptist: "Let it be so now . . . in this way to fulfill all righteousness" (Matt. 3:15). Righteousness is not an attitude or an absolute standard. It refers to conduct in accord with God's purposes. It is doing the good thing and the God thing: right doing as opposed to wrongdoing, and doing as opposed to being. Self-righteousness is the inflated ego of self-approval; righteousness is the humble ethic of living toward others in just and loving relationships. A congregation will be edified by preaching and teaching that brings righteousness into its language and life. It will be challenged to reflect on the integrity of its witness in the world. *Is* the Lord our righteousness? *Are we ready* to be named and claimed by that kind of God? *Are we willing* to welcome the day when God's justice and righteousness will be fulfilled?

DEBORAH A. BLOCK

EXEGETICAL PERSPECTIVE

Part of the climactic verses of the Little Book of Comfort, as chapters 30–33 in the book of Jeremiah have been called since Martin Luther, the lectionary passage Jeremiah 33:14–16 proclaims salvation in the form of restoration of the Davidic monarchy and pronounces a new name for Jerusalem after the Babylonian exile. The subsequent verses also promise the revival of the Levitical priesthood. Set in a part of the book of Jeremiah where destruction of the Holy City and deportation of the people to Babylon has been threatened numerous times and already taken place for the royal court and the upper classes (see the cycles of judgment oracles in Jer. 1–25 and throughout the remainder of the book), these eschatological promises of a different historical reality are spoken to give hope to a crushed people and inspire faithful endurance of the present circumstances.

How one understands what is meant by the present time and realities for Jeremiah depends on which hypothesis of composition of the book one accepts. Most biblical scholars locate the passage in exilic or postexilic writings of members of the Deuteronomistic school, who are generally considered the authors and editors of the prose sections of the book of Jeremiah during the later sixth century BCE.[6] Thus, the passage represents a vision of a radically new future added in retrospect with a postexilic audience in view. When read, however, from a literary canonical perspective,[7] the Little Book of Comfort and verses 14–16 of chapter 33 therein function as a temporary reprieve from an onslaught of judgment oracles leading up to the precise event of the destruction of the temple in Jerusalem on a particular day, the ninth of Ab in the year 587 BCE.

Opening with a formula typical of salvation oracles, "the days are surely coming," verse 14 introduces divine first-person speech. God is assuring the audience that God will fulfill "the promise," literally "the good word" with a definite article—not "a" promise, one of many, but a particular one made to both the house of Israel and the house of Judah. Harkening back to Jeremiah 23:5–6, another eschatological interlude, verse 15 reiterates what was promised there, namely, that God will birth a "righteous" (*tsedaqah*) offspring of the Davidic monarchy, who will act in ways that will promote "justice and righteousness" (*mishpat* and *tsedaqah).* While some will read this as a contradiction in terms—the Davidic monarchy has been blamed throughout the book of Jeremiah for exploitation and unfaithfulness (see Jer. 2:4–8, 26–28; 3:6–10; 7:1–15; 21:11–12)—the focus on qualities associated with the Sinai covenant, justice, and righteousness, so central to the theology and worldview of Jeremiah, does constitute something radically new in light of the present realities of destruction and impending exile.

What was promised to both Israel and Judah narrows to a promise to Judah and Jerusalem in what follows in verse 16. Both in historical and in literary terms, this makes historical sense. The Babylonian exile occurs well

6. See, e.g., Brueggemann, *A Commentary on Jeremiah.*
7. See Angela Bauer, *Gender in the Book of Jeremiah: A Feminist-Literary Reading* (New York: Peter Lang, 1999).

after the fall of the northern kingdom, so Judah and Jerusalem are at the center of the events leading up to it. Literarily, paralleling the house of Israel and the house of Judah with Judah and Jerusalem serves the movement from the bigger picture to what is at hand, the giving of a new name to the people, personified in Jerusalem. This new name is a confession of faith "YHWH is our righteousness (*tsedaqah*)." So whenever anybody utters the name of the Holy City, the person confesses his faith in the God of the covenant at Sinai. The proclamation goes even further. Given the power associated with naming in ancient Israel, giving someone or something a new name means changing them existentially. That is to say, a radical new reality is here proclaimed: the city and its people will live faithfully within the Sinai covenant by embodying its fundamental principles, justice and righteousness.

As a theological claim, such a promise goes even deeper as the new reality of a just, fair, and righteous government embraces competing theological trajectories in the First Testament—integrating the Zion covenant within the Sinai covenant.[8] This promise also fits with the more orthodox Jeremianic prophecies in particular (see Jer. 16:14–21; 23:5–8; 30:2–9; 31:1–6, 21–26, 31–34). At the same time, it joins the visions of a different way of living together as a divided people after the exile, beyond former allegiances and worldviews (see, e.g., Isa. 51:19; 54:1–17; 56:1–8; 61:1–11; Zech. 6:9–15).

By focusing on these three verses during the First Sunday of Advent, the lectionary invites the preacher and congregation to draw analogies between Jeremiah's world and contemporary dynamics locally and globally. Instances of death, destruction, and exile abound, yet particularity is encouraged. The preacher who follows the assigned text and stops with verse 16, not including the remainder of chapter 33, will want to use caution not to forget Judah's concrete historical circumstances. Jeremiah's audience is a people facing impending exile or already suffering in it. Jeremiah offers that people a vision of a radically new way their political and religious institutions may work in the future. The new generation of Davidic kings will act in ways that promote justice and righteousness, rather than exploitation, self-promotion, and violence. Further, even the Levitical priesthood will live according to the Sinai covenant, rather than continue their insistence on their own orthodoxies at the expense of inclusion, justice, and righteousness in faith and religious observance. Both king and priest someday may embody and lead the way into God's bright new reality.

Leaving out the grim present reality of soon-to-be exiles allows for a too

8. See Jon D. Levenson, *Sinai and Zion: An Entry into the Jewish Bible* (San Francisco: Harper & Row, 1985).

facile connection of the passage with the New Testament readings, which, while also eschatological in nature, presuppose a different historical context. The challenge and promise of grappling with this passage in the book of Jeremiah on the First Sunday of Advent lies in its contemporary echoes in the power structures of our time.

ANGELA BAUER-LEVESQUE

HOMILETICAL PERSPECTIVE

The season of Advent is puzzling to many Christians. The stories read during this season are, by and large, not childhood favorites. They have no star in the east guiding devout magi, no soliloquy of angels stirring shepherds to go and see the babe, no harried innkeeper, no touching moment when Mary ponders these things in her heart.

The stories of Advent are dug from the harsh soil of human struggle and the littered landscape of dashed dreams. They are told from the vista where sin still reigns supreme and hope has gone on vacation. Many prefer the major notes of joy and gladness in the Christmas stories to the minor keys of Advent.

Advent also leaves us dizzy over time. Advent is not a steady, constant, "time marches on" kind of time, a persistent drumbeat of day after day, year after year. Advent is unpredictable time, unsteady time. In this time-tumbling season, we look for a baby to be born while we know that the baby has already been born, and still is being born in us—this Emmanuel who came and is coming and is among us right now. Not only is Advent not well behaved, neat, and orderly; it contorts time. Given the nature of Advent, it is no surprise that Jeremiah is its herald.

Jeremiah speaks to hostages being seduced to start a new life in balmy Babylon. He tells a tough audience that, despite every sign to the contrary, "days are coming," days when God's promises will be fulfilled. Jeremiah tells his kin that God's future will come not by giving up on God's promises and making the best of a bad situation—after all, "when in Babylon"—but by trusting in the creative and redemptive and sure purposes of God: "Days are coming!"

With the world that he has known crumbling around him, Jeremiah pushes his people to see a future, God's future, which seems laughable given the current circumstances. No wonder Jeremiah is the church's usher into Advent. Later in the season, Mary will sing about God's future, despite her own laughable circumstance.

Along with Jeremiah and Mary, preachers would do well to consider another Advent singer. Heidi Neumark is a Lutheran pastor who writes about this holy season amid her ministry in the roughest part of the Bronx:

> Probably the reason I love Advent so much is that it is a reflection of how I feel most of the time. I might not feel sorry during Lent, when the liturgical calendar begs repentance. I might not feel victorious, even though it is Easter morning. I might not feel full of the Spirit, even though it is Pentecost and the liturgy spins out fiery gusts of ecstasy. But during Advent, I am always in sync with the season.
>
> Advent unfailingly embraces and comprehends my reality. And what is that? I think of the Spanish word *anhelo*, or longing. Advent is when the church can no longer contain its unfulfilled desire and the cry of *anhelo* bursts forth: Maranatha! Come Lord Jesus! O Come, O Come, Emmanuel![9]

As the first, lone candle of Advent wreath burns, Jeremiah recalls his own city burning, and yet he speaks not of destruction but of God's future as he offers his cry of longing, of *anhelo*. Like Jeremiah, most preachers have their own list for which they cry *anhelo*, and they serve people with their own lists of longings, for which they cry *anhelo*.

As I listen to the cries of Jeremiah throughout the scope of his prophecy, I long for the day that is surely coming when God's future will be a reality beyond the violent boastings of the ruling Babylon of the day. I long for the day that is surely coming when in God's future the poor are not sent to shelters or forced to sleep on the streets. I long for the day that is surely coming when God's future has no space for violence, when we will stop producing body bags—because there are no dead soldiers to fill them. I long for the day that is surely coming when God's future affords no room for rancor, a day when our world is no longer torn asunder by racism and sexism and homophobia.

Preaching Advent from the perspective of Jeremiah, I long for the confidence of the prophet's words about the righteous future of our God. I long for people to know the God whom Jeremiah heralds and whom Jesus will incarnate, not a hidden God who refuses to traffic in the human enterprise, but a God who hears God's people when they cry *anhelo*. I long for people to know, not the God of religious fanatics or bigots, not a God who enjoys seeing Jerusalem set afire, but the God who, in God's own time, will bring more mercy and justice than we will ever grasp.

9. Heidi Neumark, *Breathing Space* (Boston: Beacon Press, 2004), 211.

As preachers consider the prophecy from Jeremiah, maybe there is no more important homiletical clue to preaching this text than to pay attention to the *anhelo* within them and around them. Maybe, then, Jeremiah is the best biblical voice to lead us into Advent, the season that brings *anhelo* to expression.

In many liturgical traditions, the First Sunday of Advent brings the community to the holy Table. In many ways, Jeremiah's promise that "days are coming" finds its most poignant meaning at this table of *anhelo*. Just look at it. This meal does not point to magi and a star, but to a world gone mad. It is a table not cloaked in romance and sweet memories, but set with food paid for at a price way too dear. It is not just a table of *anhelo*, it is *the* table of *anhelo* for all with deep longings, people who pray with Jeremiah for the days that are surely coming.

Maybe Advent is not so puzzling after all.

GARY W. CHARLES

Luke 21:5–19

THEOLOGICAL PERSPECTIVE

Here we are invited not to be terrified (v. 9). This is possible because of the promises of God in Christ that "not a hair of your head will perish" (v. 18) and "by your endurance you will gain your souls" (v. 19). Thus we are allowed to be quietly and confidently safe in a hand that carries us. Still, it is certainly astonishing that these words are found in the biblical text for today; it is a text that is full of bad news, full of reasons that could make us timid and hopeless.

What is described in this text is similar to what happens in the windstorm that is reported to us in Matthew 8:24–26. The disciples of Jesus, together with their Master, run into the deadly danger of tempestuous waves upon the sea. As the disciples panic, Jesus lies in the boat sleeping, a sign of the heavenly peace that cannot be destroyed by any fear. Likewise, in this text, the Savior gives the same assurance to us that he gave his disciples: Be not terrified! There shall not be a hair of your head that perishes!

Indeed, even today we cannot ignore Jesus' encouragement, because it is spoken to us in an equally dangerous situation. The ground upon which we live is tottering. Securities of which we thought highly are breaking all around us. Are the words of Jesus only for the ancient world of long ago? If we think about it, we discover that Jesus' words are as relevant now as they were 2,000 years ago.

Many wars have happened since the Second World War with its millions of dead! As armies continue to be extravagantly funded, there are always new reasons to feel threatened. "Revolutions" today are called terrorism. There are "earthquakes" on the stock exchange. The polar region is melting. We are plagued by pandemics—will humans die of a virus against which we are defenseless? There are famines—great numbers of humans cannot be supplied with bread and water; do not the requirements of rich countries deprive poor countries of the possibilities for feeding themselves? Even with all the progress in 2,000 years, there are disadvantages, and do not these disadvantages have more and more of a global effect?

What can we do? An old and always new answer in such a situation says, "Let us eat and drink, for tomorrow we die" (Isa. 22:13; 1 Cor. 15:32). Do not a majority of privileged humans speak in this way today, even with the dangers of a global collapse? Such thinking is an egoistic flight from reality. Jesus shows us quite another approach in our biblical text. He says, "Not a hair of your head will perish."

In this sentence he says with cheerful confidence that our salvation lies always in good hands, in God's hands. Where there is such confidence, we are given the endurance by which we gain our souls. Such endurance requires patience, not the laziness of persons who do nothing more than "eat and drink." As legend has it, when Martin Luther was asked what he would do if he learned the world were coming to an end, he said, "If tomorrow is the Day of Judgment, then today I want to plant an apple tree."

The most evil danger is still to be highlighted. Worse than wars and earthquakes is what Jesus warns in verse 8: "Many will come in my name and say, 'I am he!' and, 'The time is near!' Do not go after them." A couple of images come to mind to illustrate Jesus' warning. A man who follows a false prophet is like a man in a plunge holding on to a seemingly secure rope, but it tears. It is like a beggar dying of starvation who receives bread, but discovers that it is in fact stone. In other words, there are persons who can tell others persuasively about Christ, but we must heed the urgent warning of the real Jesus Christ, who says, "Do not listen to those so-called preachers in my name. Do not follow them. They seem to save from ruin, but in fact they lead to it."

The Russian writer Dostoevsky has written a dismaying story with the title "The Grand Inquisitor." It concerns an old cardinal of the Christian church who hears that the real Jesus has come suddenly to his town, where he has healed a blind man and raised a young girl from the dead. When the cardinal sees this, he asks him: "Why, then, have you come to interfere with us?" The cardinal would like to burn him at a funeral pyre as the most evil of all heretics, because what he did long ago is done far better by the church today. The church does not need him, even if it is called by his name. However, the cardinal does say: "'Go and do not come again . . . do not come at all . . . never, never!'" And he lets him out into the dark 'square of the city.'"[10] Dostoevsky illustrates this sentence of Jesus: "Many will come in my name, claiming, 'I am he!' . . . Do not go after them" (v. 8).

What can help us in the face of such an earnest threat? It is important that we live by what is said at the beginning of this essay. In the face of such threat, there is no technique that we may learn from Jesus and put into practice by ourselves. Our help is from the Helper himself. Jesus gives us the promise that he watches over us so that "not a hair of [our] head will perish" (v. 18). Without him holding our hands, we would be lost or like that apparently pious cardinal. While our Lord holds us, we are able to cling to him and to his word: "So make up your minds not to prepare your defense in advance; for I will give you words and a wisdom that none of your opponents will be able to withstand or contradict" (vv. 14–15).

EBERHARD BUSCH

PASTORAL PERSPECTIVE

Every generation, at some time in its history, has thought its time was the end of time—and the dawn of the twenty-first century has been no exception. The current generation can reflect upon experiences of war, natural disaster, and political chaos as fodder for apocalyptic possibility.

Most people remember where they were and what they were doing on September 11, 2001, when nineteen terrorists associated with Al-Qaeda hijacked four commercial airline jets. The sight of hundreds of military tanks streaming across the desert toward Baghdad as part of the "shock and awe" campaign is emblazoned on the American imagination. On December 26, 2004, the world was startled by a tsunami in Indonesia, one of the deadliest natural disasters in history. Many people have vivid memories of news footage from New Orleans during and after Hurricane Katrina. While it is not clear that these and other phenomena are in any way apocalyptic (only God knows the end time), Jesus' directions to the disciples concerning what they ought to do in times of chaos and destruction were quite challenging then, and are equally challenging for us today.

In Luke 21:5–6 Jesus speaks of the destruction of the temple, prompting the disciples to ask two questions: When? What will be the sign? Jesus

---

10. Fyodor Dostoevsky, *The Brothers Karamazov*, trans. Richard Pevear and Larissa Volokhonsky (New York: Alfred A. Knopf Everyone's Library, 1992), 250 and 262.

goes on to describe three things that will happen in the future (vv. 8–11): imposters will come and try to trick the faithful; war and conflict will rage on; and natural disasters will be prevalent. Jesus assures the disciples that the end times are in the future and that they will not happen all at once. Then Jesus says a rather peculiar thing in verse 13: "This will give you an opportunity to testify."

He goes on to tell the disciples that their testimony must not be rehearsed or "canned." Instead, they should rely on the incontestable wisdom that will be given them in the moment. Jesus says that the reward for their testimony and their endurance of these catastrophic times will be the gaining of their very souls. Let us reflect on Jesus' peculiar statement about suffering as opportunity for testimony.

What kind of testimony does a faithful person give in the face of death, betrayal, and the execution of loved ones? Most of us are accustomed to testimonies that praise God for good times, good things, blessings of redemption, healing, rescue, and salvation. Testimony is usually reserved for the stories that declare how God brought the faithful out of slavery into freedom, how God made a way when there was no way; how God acted to save a distressed people. The peculiar words of Jesus in this passage, however, tell us that when we experience destruction, betrayal, and loss, we are to see these times as opportunities to testify. What kind of testimony does one give in the face of great suffering and great hatred?

"Suffering always means pain, disruption, separation, and incompleteness," writes Shawn Copeland. "It can render us powerless and mute, push us to the borders of hopelessness and despair."[11] The opportunity to testify during times of destruction is, in part, the audacity to muster courage in the face of fear, the boldness to speak in the face of suffering. Great suffering changes some people and defeats others, but for those who endure—their very souls are gained.

Suffering provides an opportunity for those who have been changed to tell of their hope. For some, the change brought about by suffering is tangible, literal, physical. Howard Thurman, brilliant African American theologian, has seen suffering change people: "Into their faces come a subtle radiance and a settled serenity; into their relationships a vital generosity that opens the sealed doors of the heart in all who are encountered along the way."[12]

---

11. M. Shawn Copeland, "Wading through Many Sorrows: Toward a Theology of Suffering in Womanist Perspective," in *A Troubling in My Soul: Womanist Perspectives on Evil and Suffering* (Maryknoll, NY: Orbis, 1993), 109.
12. Howard Thurman, *Disciplines of the Spirit* (1963; Richmond, IN: Friends United Press, 1977), 76.

An opportunity for testimony born out of a time of loss, grief, and chaos is recorded in the song "Precious Lord," written by Thomas Dorsey. Thomas Dorsey, born in 1889 in rural Georgia, was a prolific songwriter and an excellent gospel and blues musician. While a young man, Dorsey moved to Chicago and found work as a piano player in the churches as well as in clubs and playing in theatres. Struggling to support his family, Dorsey divided his time between playing in the clubs and playing in the church. After some time of turbulence, Dorsey devoted his artistry exclusively to the church.

In August of 1932, Dorsey left his pregnant wife in Chicago and traveled to be the featured soloist at a large revival meeting in St. Louis. After the first night of the revival, Dorsey received a telegram that simply said, "Your wife just died." Dorsey raced home and learned that his wife had given birth to a son before dying in childbirth. The next day his son died as well. Dorsey buried his wife and son in the same casket and withdrew in sorrow and agony from his family and friends. He refused to compose or play any music for quite some time.

While still in the midst of despair, Dorsey said that as he sat in front of a piano, a feeling of peace washed through him. He heard a melody in his head that he had never heard before and began to play it on the piano. That night, Dorsey recorded this testimony while in the midst of suffering:

Precious Lord, take my hand,
Lead me on, let me stand;
I am tired, I am weak, I am worn;
Through the storm, through the night,
Lead me on to the light;
Take my hand, precious Lord,
Lead me home.[13]

NANCY LYNNE WESTFIELD

EXEGETICAL PERSPECTIVE

The Jerusalem Temple, Worldly Turmoil, and Persecution. As the scene opens, Jesus engages in public dialogue with people about the beautiful Jerusalem temple (vv. 5–7). As it continues, Jesus presents a monologue about future times of false leadership, violence, and suffering (vv. 8–11), about arrest, persecution, and endurance (vv. 12–19), and about destruction of Jerusalem that signals the eventual coming of the Son of Man (vv. 20–36).

13. Thomas A. Dorsey, "Precious Lord, Take My Hand," in *The Presbyterian Hymnal* (Louisville, KY: Westminster/John Knox Press, 1990), 404. See also http://www.pbs.org/ thisfarbyfaith/people/thomas_dorsey.html (PBS—*This Far by Faith: Series on People of Faith—Thomas Dorsey*).

Future Destruction of the Temple (vv. 5–6). The magnificent temple in Jerusalem during the lifetime of Jesus was the result of a rebuilding project started by King Herod in 19 BCE. Herod more than doubled the size of the Temple Mount. People could gather in large colonnades or porches around the Temple Mount for various purposes, including speech making and healing (see Acts 3:11; 5:12). While the temple itself was completed in eighteen months, work on the outer courts and decorations continued throughout Jesus' lifetime until 62–64 CE.

Less than a decade after everything was completed on the Herodian temple, it was destroyed by the Romans in 70 CE. The descriptive language in Luke 21:5 exhibits widespread knowledge of its beauty and magnificence. After its destruction, people knew about its magnificence all the way to Rome, as a result of the exhibition of the plundered furnishings and the large paintings of the events of the Roman siege and burning of Jerusalem that were paraded on wagons in a triumphal procession in Rome in 71 CE (Josephus, *Wars* 7.3–5). In the Gospels, the destruction is described as "not one stone will be left upon another; all will be thrown down" (v. 6). When Jerusalem and its temple were destroyed in 70 CE, Christians considered this a confirmation of a prediction Jesus had made during his lifetime.

False Leadership (vv. 7–8). During the time leading up to the destruction of Jerusalem, many people either took action to defy the governing powers or were suspected of doing so and were destroyed by Herodian or Roman soldiers. A current Web site lists fifteen leaders between 4 BCE and 70 CE who were perceived to have defied the Romans and were destroyed.[14] Verse 8 quotes Jesus as saying that the appearance of various leaders, some claiming to be Jesus or at least divine ("I am he!") and some predicting the end of time, will be the first sign that the destruction of the Jerusalem temple will soon take place (v. 7). Luke's Gospel presupposes that the appearance of various leaders who were captured, imprisoned, and/or killed confirmed Jesus' view of events that would happen before the destruction of Jerusalem and its temple.

War and World Turbulence (vv. 9–11). After Jesus warns about people who will come to lead them astray, he describes terrible events that grow ever greater in magnitude. In the Lukan account, these are not "the beginnings of the birth pangs" (Matt. 24:8; Mark 13:8). Rather, these events represent

14. http://www.livius.org/men-mh/messiah/messianic_claimants00.html. The list of fifteen includes Jesus.

the turmoil that will increase until the destruction of Jerusalem and its temple. First there will be wars and insurrections (v. 9). This may refer to the rapid succession of four Roman emperors in 69 CE prior to the siege and destruction of Jerusalem. Second, nations and kingdoms will rise up against one another (v. 10). Instead of making this warfare a transition to end-time events (cf. Matt. 24:7; Mark 13:8), the Lukan account makes it the next step in the process that leads to the attack on Jerusalem. Third, there will be great earthquakes, and in some places famines and plagues (v. 11a). Luke's own account of the time between Jesus and the destruction of Jerusalem presents a famine in the time of Claudius (Acts 11:28; ca. 47 CE) and an earthquake in Philippi (Acts 16:26; ca. 50 CE). Fourth, "there will be dreadful portents and great signs from heaven" (v. 11b). Scholars have noticed that Josephus's account of a star resembling a sword and a comet at the burning of the Jerusalem temple (*War* 6.289) is similar to the conclusion of the Lukan sequence of events. Jesus' speech in Luke, then, focuses first on the destruction of Jerusalem and its temple, rather than on the end of time.

Arrest, Persecution, Hatred, and Endurance (vv. 12–19). In Luke's account, Jesus does not present suffering and persecution as part of the tribulations that lead up to the end time (cf. Matt. 24:9–14; Mark 13:9–13). Rather, Jesus says that arrests, persecution, trials, betrayal by family members, and hatred against them will all occur before the sequence of turmoil that leads to the destruction of Jerusalem and the temple (v. 12), which the author knows occurred in 70 CE, about twenty years before he wrote his Gospel. This means that verses 12–19 refer to events like those one reads about in the Acts of the Apostles, which is the second volume Luke wrote sometime after completing the Gospel of Luke.

In Luke's historical theology, the time of the church is a time when people who endure will "gain [their] souls" (v. 19). Matthew 24:13 and Mark 13:13, in contrast, feature Jesus saying that those who endure to the end will be saved. The Lukan account has Jesus describe the destruction of Jerusalem in terms close to the way it happened, namely, being "surrounded by armies" (v. 20) as Rome enacted "days of vengeance" against a rebellious population (v. 22). In a similar way, it has Jesus describe the sufferings and hardships of his followers in terms Luke uses in Acts. Jesus' followers will be arrested (v. 12a; cf. Acts 4:3; 5:18; 12:1; 21:27). They also will be "handed over" to authorities (v. 12b; cf. Acts 21:11; 28:17). They will testify before kings and governors (vv. 12–13; cf. Acts 24–26) and present wisdom that others will not be able to withstand (v. 15; cf. Stephen in Acts 6:10). In Luke's account of Jesus' speech, then, the emphasis in the initial part is not on the coming of the end time but on events that happened in the lives of followers of Jesus through the time of the destruction of Jerusalem and its temple.

VERNON K. ROBBINS

HOMILETICAL PERSPECTIVE

Luke's account of Jesus' teaching in 21:5–19 provides a cluttered text full of disorientation, dismaying ideas, and distractions aplenty.

The disciples begin distracted. They marvel at the beauty of the temple, the enormous stones of its walls, and the wealthy worshipers coming to dedicate their gifts. Small wonder they are distracted. The public exhibition of fabulous wealth has a way of distracting us, whether we see it in *Town and Country* or *People* magazine, and the temple was Herod's temple, the jewel in his architectural crown. The New Testament remembers Herod as a paranoid despot, but history and archaeologists remember him as a builder. In the church library there is probably a volume that includes an artist's rendering of Herod's temple. Look it up: you will be impressed too. Everyone was.

Perhaps not everyone. Jesus interrupts his disciples' distraction by hanging out a sign naming everything that so dazzles them as "Condemned Property." The enormous stones, beautiful, smooth, and apparently indestructible: "not one stone will be left upon another"; the glorious temple dedicated to a glorious God (but also filled with graft [20:47]): "all will be thrown down" (v. 8).

Writing sometime after the destruction of the temple, Luke characterizes Jesus as a reliable prophet whose words were proven true by historical events. Those who listen to him discover that all of Jesus' words are true, and therefore listeners can trust these words that threaten such dismaying dislocations.

Theologically Luke means to distinguish the end time of all things from particular historical events. The temple may have come to an end, but that is not *the* end; peace will come to an end and be swallowed by war, but war is not the way the world ends; security will end, shaken in earthquakes, but fear and uncertainty are not the end either. People will try to mimic Jesus and misuse his name attempting to prophesy as he did, but the world does not end with truth's impersonators. "Dreadful portents and great signs from heaven" (v. 11) may tempt you to play prophet yourself, reading the concealed meanings of mysterious happenings, but knowing the end does not belong to you (cf. Acts 1:7; 1 Thess. 5:1–11). Theologically Luke no doubt has an important point to make, but rhetorically he frightens his readers to their wits' ends.

Wars, insurrections, earthquakes, famine, plagues, and, just when it seems it cannot possibly get any worse, it gets personal: *You* will be arrested, *you* will be persecuted, *you* will be thrown into prison and hauled before the authorities. Then, Jesus says, then you will have them right where you want them. They will have to listen to you. Just when everything looks so dark, when falsehood appears so persuasive, when war seems everlasting and inevitable, when the earth trembles beneath you, when you are forced to account for yourself, you have "an opportunity to testify" (v. 13).

This rambling, discombobulated directory of events—wars, earthquakes, famine—these are not random happenings, nor are they reliable signs of the end, but they are things that *must* first happen in the grand design of God's redemption (v. 9, the divine imperative *dei:* "these things *must* take place first"). We had not noticed the plan. The sheer immensity of wars, earthquakes, famine, and plagues so completely arrests our attention that we seldom look for something even more overwhelming. In Jesus' vision, however, these dramatic historical events are simply a required stage setting for the great drama of speaking God's truth.

Given the towering backdrop of wars, earthquakes, and famine, we might assume we do not have much to say. Moreover, arrest, persecution, and arraignment notoriously intimidate and silence people. Everything, however, is working according to plan, God's plan: "This will give you an opportunity to testify" (v. 13). If we must speak we should like some time to prepare, to consult perhaps a volume like this and to arrange our thoughts, but Jesus dismisses our anxiety as unnecessary. Our powerlessness to speak may be our most essential qualification.

For those who do not know what to say at a crucial moment, conventional wisdom provides maxims like "Don't worry, it will come to you!" and "You'll be just fine; you'll think of something at the last moment!" Those folk anodynes are precisely what Jesus does not offer those compelled to speak. Instead, he promises them, "I will give you words." The words we have to say we receive as a gift. Christ possesses a wisdom our troubled world and his troubling opponents cannot calculate or comprehend. Although they have rejected his words before, once again Christ will speak the word of the kingdom through his church.

Christ promises to speak the word, which is to say we do not have to create these words. The word we are given is the word that created all things in the beginning (Gen. 1:3; John 1:1–3) and continues to create in its speaking. We do not speak with confidence but rather out of our speaking and hearing ourselves bear testimony we receive the gift of faith: "Faith comes from what is heard, and what is heard comes through the word of Christ" (Rom. 10:17). Such is the power of Jesus' words that they not only describe a kingdom but fashion a habitable place. The disclosures of Luke 21:5–19 take their own opportunity to testify to this.

Just as the destruction of the temple testified to the truthfulness of Jesus' words when the Gospel of Luke was written, so do these words spoken in the worship of Christian communities bear witness to Christ's unshakable promise. They are only words, small breaths of air spoken millennia ago, but these words endure with power, even power to "gain your souls" (v. 19). The temple is destroyed, not one stone left on another. The Roman Empire collapsed into history. These words endure, and their promise is not diminished by earthquake, war, or famine—or even by the passing of years.

PATRICK J. WILLSON

Second Sunday of Advent

Malachi 3:1–4

¹See, I am sending my messenger to prepare the way before me, and the Lord whom you seek will suddenly come to his temple. The messenger of the covenant in whom you delight—indeed, he is coming, says the LORD of hosts. ²But who can endure the day of his coming, and who can stand when he appears?

For he is like a refiner's fire and like fullers' soap; ³he will sit as a refiner and purifier of silver, and he will purify the descendants of Levi and refine them like gold and silver, until they present offerings to the LORD in righteousness. ⁴Then the offering of Judah and Jerusalem will be pleasing to the LORD as in the days of old and as in former years.

Matthew 24:36–44

³⁶"But about that day and hour no one knows, neither the angels of heaven, nor the Son, but only the Father. ³⁷For as the days of Noah were, so will be the coming of the Son of Man. ³⁸For as in those days before the flood they were eating and drinking, marrying and giving in marriage, until the day Noah entered the ark, ³⁹and they knew nothing until the flood came and swept them all away, so too will be the coming of the Son of Man. ⁴⁰Then two will be in the field; one will be taken and one will be left. ⁴¹Two women will be grinding meal together; one will be taken and one will be left. ⁴²Keep awake therefore, for you do not know on what day your Lord is coming. ⁴³But understand this: if the owner of the house had known in what part of the night the thief was coming, he would have stayed awake and would not have let his house be broken into. ⁴⁴Therefore you also must be ready, for the Son of Man is coming at an unexpected hour.

ORDER OF WORSHIP

OPENING WORDS / CALL TO WORSHIP

The Lord is coming to his temple. *Mal. 3:1*

We watch and wait for his coming. *Matt. 24:42–44*

Prepare the way of the Lord! *Mal. 3:1*

LIGHTING OF THE ADVENT CANDLES

    [Reader 1]: We light this candle as a symbol of the
                 purity of heart only God can bring.

    [Reader 2]: For he shall purify his people like gold
                 and silver, until they shine forth his righteousness.

    [All]: **Come, Lord Jesus, come!**

HYMN, SPIRITUAL, OR PSALM

CALL TO CONFESSION

Saints, let us trust in God's love for us and
    confess our sin,
confident in God's mercy.

PRAYER OF CONFESSION

Refining God, you have sent us prophets and
    we have not listened. *Mal. 3:1–2*
We have not always determined what is best
or made way for your reign
in our lives, our church, and our society.
Forgive us, we pray, and renew your covenant
    within us,
for the sake of Jesus Christ, our Lord. Amen.

DECLARATION OF FORGIVENESS

Friends, I am confident of this:
if we repent, God is sure to forgive us.
The One who began a good work in us will
    bring it to completion.
Grateful for the promise of joy and of peace,
let us share that peace with one another.

PRAYER OF THE DAY

Covenant God,
you send us messengers   *Mal. 3:1–3*
to cleanse and refine us for your coming.
Help us endure the mirror of the prophets' message,
that we may see you when you suddenly appear
    among us;
through Jesus Christ. **Amen.**

HYMN, SPIRITUAL, OR PSALM

PRAYER FOR ILLUMINATION

Holy One, through your Holy Spirit
instruct us by the light of your prophets.
Illumine our hearts, that we may hear your call
to become your path into the world.
In the name of Jesus Christ we pray. **Amen.**

SCRIPTURE READINGS

SERMON

HYMN, SPIRITUAL, OR PSALM

PRAYERS OF INTERCESSION

Sisters and brothers in Christ,
for the sake of the world that God so loves, let us pray.

Pray for the peace of Jerusalem.
We pray for peace in every nation—
that hatred and ill will in the hearts of all people,
will be burned away in your refining fire,
leaving only love.   *Mal. 3:2*

Pray for the peace of the church.
We pray for peace in Christ's body—
put an end to fear and fighting,
that we may proclaim your good news
and be awake to your presence.   *Matt. 24:42–44*

Pray for the peace of this community.
We pray for peace in this place—
for safety in our homes and streets,
for the prosperity of our neighbors,
and for the health of family and friends.

God of the future,   *Matt. 24:37*
make us ready for the coming of your reign,
when you will bring everlasting peace
and renew the face of the earth;
through Jesus Christ our Lord. **Amen.**

LORD'S PRAYER

INVITATION TO THE OFFERING
Present offerings to the Lord in righteousness.   *Mal. 3:3*
Give with pure hearts

PRAYER OF THANKSGIVING/DEDICATION
God of all righteousness,   *Mal. 3:1–4*
receive these gifts of gratitude,
the offerings of our lives.
Purify them with your refining fire
so that they may serve your purposes
and shine with your glory;
through Jesus Christ our Lord. **Amen.**

HYMN, SPIRITUAL, OR PSALM

CHARGE
About that day and hour no one knows.   *Matt. 24:36, 42, 44*
Therefore keep awake,
for you do not know on what day your Lord
    is coming.
Be ready, for the Lord will come at an
    unexpected hour.

BLESSING
May the Spirit of the Lord surround you
as you walk and wait for his coming.

SONG SUGGESTIONS

"Come Down, O Love Divine" (*ELW* 804, *GC* 465, *GTG* 282, *TNCH* 289, *UMH* 475)

"Come, Thou Long-Expected Jesus" (*CH* 125, *EH* 66, *ELW* 254, *GC* 323, *GTG* 82–83, *TNCH* 122, *UMH* 196)

"Comfort, Comfort Now My People" (*CH* 122–123, *EH* 67, *ELW* 256, *GC* 326, *GTG* 87, *TNCH* 101)

"Jesus, Thine All-Victorious Love" (*UMH* 422)

"Light One Candle to Watch for Messiah," stanza 2 (*ELW* 240, *GTG* 85)

"O Come, O Come, Emmanuel" (*CH* 119, *ELW* 257, *GC* 317, *GTG* 88, *TNCH* 116, *UMH* 211)

"People, Look East" (*CH* 142, *ELW* 248, *GC* 318, *GTG* 105, *UMH* 202)

"While We Are Waiting, Come" (*GTG* 92)

CHILDREN'S SERMON

Based on Malachi 3:1–4

During Advent, we are getting ready for Jesus to be born. We talked last week about how God sent messengers called prophets to help the people get ready for God to come to earth. One of these messengers was called Malachi, which means "my messenger." We don't know if this was his real name or if he was just such a great messenger that that is what they called him.

Malachi knew that the people were not ready for God to come. They were not behaving like God wanted them to. They cheated and lied and treated people badly. God wanted them to give the best of what they had as an offering, and instead they gave God the yucky stuff they did not want. This made God sad. God loved them and knew they could be good, with some help. So he gave Malachi a message for the people.

Like most people, these people were not all bad. They had good in them, all mixed up with the bad. So Malachi told them they were like precious metal pulled out of the ground—very special, but with a lot of bad mixed in with the good. Gold and silver come out of the ground in chunks of rock. It is not very pretty and has a bunch of other types of metal and rock mixed in. God is sending someone, Malachi said, who will be like a refiner and purifier of gold. A refiner heats up the mixed-up metal with a very hot fire, melts it down, and cleans out the stuff that is not pure gold. With all that stuff cleaned out, the gold can be pure and shiny.

Malachi told the people, "God will send someone to take away the bad stuff and make what is good in you even better. Then you will be like pure and shiny gold, and your whole life will be a good offering for God."

Prayer: Thank you for the prophets, who told us how you wanted us to live. Amen.

SERMON HELPS

Malachi 3:1–4

THEOLOGICAL PERSPECTIVE

Despite all of the ambiguities regarding the date and authorship of Malachi, most scholars agree that this minor prophet was speaking to a postexilic community of Jews who had returned to Judah. Much of the book is written as a series of *disputations*, and the prophet serves as an arbiter in these conflicts between the people and God. In response to complaints that God has failed to exercise divine judgment, the prophet delivers an eschatological rebuttal, which raises several points with significant theological import. This essay will address two broad themes, which the reader finds woven together throughout the lection: (1) divine judgment, the Day of the Lord, and the character of God's justice, and (2) the purification of the people.

Divine Judgment, the Day of the Lord, and the Character of God's Justice. The people, newly restored in Judah, are skeptical of God's justice, because their practices of piety have yielded neither divine retributive judgment against "evildoers" nor prosperity for the restoration community. Their challenges to the prophet smack of self-righteousness, and they seemingly have failed to notice that their compromised worship practices, marital infidelity, and social injustice dishonor God. They seek and desire the coming of the Lord, imagining that it will be favorable for them. The prophet, however, reminds the people that the arrival of divine judgment rarely meets human expectations—it is sudden, surprising, and often as much a judgment against the ones yearning for it as it is a judgment against their enemies (Amos 5:18). When the Day of the Lord arrives, the prophet warns, all will be found guilty and all will be deserving of punishment. In particular, in verse 5 (curiously, not part of this lection), the prophet warns that God's swift judgment will be executed upon the perpetrators of social injustice.

God's judgment should not, however, be understood as solely punitive, even though the people seem to deserve punishment. God's justice is not the justice expected by the restoration community. Instead, in this text we find that the divine judgment to be exercised on the Day of the Lord has a more long-range telos, in that it will issue in a process of purification that makes a place hospitable for the abiding presence of God. In the end, God's schema of justice is restorative rather than retributive.

The Purification of the People. In two places in this short lection, we find references to the ways in which purifying preparations are made for God's presence with the people. In verse 1, the prophet points to the coming of a messenger who would clear or "prepare the way of the Lord." In verses 2–3, the prophet describes the Lord's coming as like the refiner's fire, whose purpose is to remove impurities and strengthen the substance being refined. John Calvin wrote this about the refiner's fire: "The power of the fire, we know, is twofold: for it burns and it purifies; it burns what is corrupt; but it purifies gold and silver from their dross."

The refiner's fire has made a number of appearances in theological discourse over time. What is it that stands in need of purification? And what will be consumed by flames in the process? After purification, what is it that God reckons as precious metal? Calvin thought that the refiner's fire would serve to correct the corruption not only of the people, but of the Levitical priests also: "Such then was the contagion, that not only the common people became corrupt, but even the Levites themselves, who ought to have been guides to others, and who were to be in the Church as it were the pattern of holiness. God however promises that such would be the purifying which Christ would effect, and so regulated, that it would consume the whole people, and yet purify the elect, and purify them like silver, that they may be saved."[1]

Two things should be said about Calvin's interpretation of verse 3 and the association he makes with the *doctrine of election*. First, Calvin's commentaries on the prophets, not surprisingly, have a christocentric focus that sometimes crosses over into a supersessionist interpretation. We must always exercise a bit of caution, then, when consulting these texts, even when we do so in the context of Advent, a time in the liturgical year particularly set aside for the anticipation of the coming Messiah. Second, even as Calvin derives support for the doctrine of election in the Malachi passage, he also reminds the reader that election is not for privilege, but for a purpose. Once again,

1. John Calvin, *Commentaries on the Twelve Minor Prophets*, vol. 5, ed. and trans. John Owen (Grand Rapids: Eerdmans, 1950), 573.

proper temple worship would be restored, and the people (Levitical priests, in particular) would make offerings acceptable to God.

Purification has another possible purpose, as well, in addition to the removal of impurities. When silver is refined, it is treated with carbon or charcoal, preventing the absorption of oxygen and resulting in its sheen and purity. One writer has suggested that a silversmith knows that the refining process is complete only when she observes her "own image reflected in the mirror-like surface of the metal."[2] If this is the case, does the prophet also suggest that the *imago Dei* is restored in this process? Is humanity deemed good and righteous when once again the divine image is reflected in the human heart?[3]

JENNIFER RYAN AYRES

PASTORAL PERSPECTIVE

Years ago I heard Elie Weisel, the Jewish writer and Nobel Prize winner, recall a childhood story. When he was a boy, his mother would greet him every day when he returned from school. Every day she would ask him the same question. She did not ask, "What did you do today?" or "Whom did you talk to today?" or even "What did you learn today?" She would ask, "Did you have a good question today?"

Malachi had some good questions for his day. How has God loved us? (1:2) "Has not one God created us?" (2:10) "Where is the God of justice?" (2:17) How shall we return to God? (3:7) Malachi poses twenty-two questions in just fifty-five verses. God's questions to the priests and the people are articulated; their responses to God are anticipated. Rhetorical questions emphasize the prophetic passion for integrity; direct inquiries evoke the people's questions and provoke impassioned response. The question-and-answer style opens prophetic deliverance to more of a prophet-and-people deliberation, edgy but candid, confrontational and engaging. They are now partners in critical reflection on the nature of God and self-critical reflection on the conduct of Israel.

Malachi has some good questions for our day. His very use of questions as a means of prophetic revelation counters the unthinking certitude of much so-called religious conviction. "Who can endure the day of his coming?" (3:2) Who will be "pure and blameless" in the day of Christ? (Phil.

---

2. Ralph L. Smith, *Micah-Malachi*, Word Bible Commentary 32 (Waco, TX: Word Books, 1984), 329.
3. Calvin famously likened the *imago Dei* to a mirror within the human soul, which is meant to reflect God's glory (*Institutes of the Christian Religion*, ed. John McNeil, trans. Ford Lewis Battles [Philadelphia:Westminster Press, 1960], 1.15.4).

1:10) Who will prepare the way by repentance and forgiveness? (Luke 3:1–6) Advent questions! Advent questions our worthiness, readiness, and willingness for Christ's coming. "The descendants of Levi" are called to new "integrity and uprightness," a turning "from iniquity," and a renewed "reverence" for God's "covenant of life and well-being" with us (Mal. 2:5–6). Like the ancient priesthood, the contemporary priesthood of believers opens its life to the refining presence of God and offers its life in righteous practice.

A faithful hearing of this text will turn the church to some good questions about its worship life during Advent: Are prayers prophetic as well as personal, directed to injustice and corruption as well as seasonal anxiety and individual omissions? Today's prayer of confession admits, "Refining God, you have sent us prophets and we have not listened." Another prayer asks, "Help us endure the mirror of the prophets' message, that we may see you when you suddenly appear among us."

Is the Word proclaimed through the sacrament of baptism? The baptismal liturgy poses some good questions. Malachi's indictment that "you have turned aside from the way" (2:8) and John's "baptism of repentance for the forgiveness of sins" (Luke 3:3) are echoed in the profession of faith. "Trusting in the gracious mercy of God, do you turn from the ways of sin and renounce evil and its power in the world?" Malachi's image of God's messenger as "fullers' soap" who "will purify the descendants of Levi" (3:2b–3) is reflected in the Thanksgiving over the Water when we praise God for giving us a "cleansing and rebirth . . . that we might . . . serve you as a royal priesthood."[4] The communal significance of baptism involves the entire congregation in reaffirming God's "covenant of life and well-being" in Jesus Christ. Baptism prepares the way, and it answers one of Malachi's most pressing questions: "Where is the God of justice?" (2:17). Today's text begins an answer. "See, I am sending my messenger to prepare the way." The sacrament of baptism is a sign that God is here, with us, in the world.

Do hymns and choral music express the messenger's judgment as well as the joy? While many are eager to sing and hear the familiar Christmas carols, Advent hymn themes are discordant, unsung, and unpopular in many congregations. The notes of today's lectionary texts are sounded in hymns like "O Day of God, Draw Near," which sings of judgment and faithfulness, justice and security.[5]

---

4. *Book of Common Worship* (Louisville, KY: Westminster/John Knox Press, 1993), 407, 411.
5. *The New Century Hymnal* (Cleveland: The Pilgrim Press, 1995), 611; *The Presbyterian Hymnal* (Louisville, KY: Westminster/John Knox Press, 1990), 452.

The text of Malachi 3:1–3 appears in one of the signature choral works of this season, George Frideric Handel's *Messiah*. With his libretto, Charles Jennens raised Malachi's faithful question about the nature of God's love. He answered it with a catena of powerful Scriptures. A congregation blessed with the choral acumen to offer this masterpiece should hear the Malachi text in context. The recitative ("The Lord, whom ye seek shall suddenly come"), air for bass ("But who may abide the day of his coming?") and chorus ("He shall purify the sons of Levi") is answered by an alto, "Behold, a virgin shall conceive, and bear a Son, and shall call his name Emmanuel, God with us." Music can sing the Word and proclaim the good news.

On this Second Sunday of Advent, music can sing the Word, proclaim the good news, and challenge both preacher and congregation. After the first presentation of *Messiah* in London in 1741, Handel wrote to a friend: "I should be sorry if I only entertained them. I wished to make them better." The composer challenges the preacher to go beyond feeling good to doing good. At issue are some good questions about worship in our day: Entertainment or edification? Diversion or direction? Amusement or awareness? Handel himself provided an answer. Although by 1751 he was blind, until his death he conducted *Messiah* as an annual benefit for the Foundling Hospital in London, which served mostly widows and orphans of the clergy. The intent was not just to entertain; Handel's hope was to make them just and better. His ear was open to the prophetic word: "Present offerings to the LORD in righteousness" (Mal. 3:3).

Malachi opens the church to some good questions for today.

DEBORAH A. BLOCK

EXEGETICAL PERSPECTIVE

The short biblical book of Malachi hails from the Second Temple period, also known as postexilic times, and was written clearly after the dedication of the Second Temple in 515 BCE (see Ezra 6:15). Lamenting the corruption of the priesthood, its author must have lived long enough after the initial celebration and dedication to allow for the witness of discontent and questionable ritual practices (Mal. 1:6–14), somewhere in the first half of the fifth century BCE. Malachi, the Hebrew word for "my messenger," may be the self-designation of a priest disgruntled with the practices of his colleagues and congregation, rather than a personal name; alternatively, it may be a pun on such a name. While some ancient sources assume that the messenger is Ezra (see Targum; also *b. Meg.* 15a), others have identified him as Mordecai (Rabbi Nachman). Yet others wonder whether this was a reference to the prophet Elijah (see Mal. 4:5–6). Prophesying from the center of religious (and by extension some social) power, this temple prophet identifies with divine first-person speech, calling other priests and the people to account.[6]

This lection follows Malachi's poignant questions of dysfunctional religion by means of rhetorical questions about the people's accountability to the covenant and the implied lack thereof, which ignorantly ask where to find the God of justice (Mal. 2:17). The prophet switches his tone in 3:1–4 while continuing the judgment oracle, which is the fourth of six oracles in the book (1:2–5; 1:6–2:9; 2:10–16; 2:17–3:5; 3:6–12; 3:13–4:3). Alternating between first- and third-person divine speech, the passage talks about a future time, characterized as a day of judgment (Mal. 3:5). Language reminiscent of Second Isaiah (see Isa. 40:3) proclaims the commission of God's messenger "to prepare the way before me" to usher in the sudden arrival of God in the temple. This staging of a grand entrance for YHWH at a time of discontent and disappointment, in the midst of struggles for direction among those who find themselves back in Judah, utilizes the memory of comfort and liberation from a century earlier to invoke the possibility of another change in direction.

The passage continues with *YHWH Zebaoth*, the God of hosts, promising the arrival of "the messenger of the covenant" with the attribute "in whom you delight" (Mal. 3:1b). This attribute is a formula used for both God and human beings throughout the First Testament (see Deut. 10:15; Gen. 34:19; 1 Sam. 18:22; Pss. 5:5; 34:13; etc.). While much more prevalent in its absence, its presence indicates a specially sanctioned event. So what is going on in this grand entrance, and who is really arriving? The text remains ambiguous as to whether the reference is to a messenger, who may or may not be identical with the messenger of the covenant mentioned in the following sentence, or to God, or to the "great king" promised in Malachi 1:14. Commentators through the ages have debated the identity of this messenger, including the possibility of a priestly messiah figure. Centuries later, in the New Testament the Malachi verse is merged with the verse in Second Isaiah to identify the messenger with John the Baptizer (Matt. 11:10; Mark 1:2; Luke 7:27).

While the actual identity of this ominous figure remains vague, its impact is not. This messenger is to enforce the covenant with powerful means, "like a refiner's fire and like fullers' soap" (Mal. 3:2). It is not just any fire and any soap, but very particular ones, resulting in a particular process of cleansing. Such purification will be characterized by extreme heat and strong lye;

6. See for example, Eileen M. Schuller, OSU, "The Book of Malachi: Introduction, Commentary, and Reflections," in *The New Interpreter's Bible*, vol. 7 (Nashville: Abingdon Press, 1996), 841–77.

all possible uncleanliness will be burned and washed away from the Levitical priesthood until the ideal of covenant faithfulness is demonstrated by their performance of "offerings in righteousness" (Mal. 3:3). Righteousness (*tsedaqah*) is an essential quality of the covenant made with Moses and the people at Sinai (see Exod. 19:1–6). This covenant, the ideal of Torah living, is held up by the majority of the prophets. Thus, to these idealized times of the past, Malachi calls this Second-Temple people to return (Mal. 3:4).

Read thusly, the message of these verses is basically a conservative one, as it calls for a return to the idealized past to avoid the threat of judgment. The "good old times" are invoked and promised as a possibility, if only the people and the priesthood change their current ways: this is what a simplistic reading would suggest.

To arrive at a more differentiated interpretation of the present-past-future continuum in Malachi and other prophetic books of the Second Temple period, one needs to consider the sociohistorical context of the Judeans under the Persian Empire.[7] A mixed multitude of those who returned from the exile in Babylon, those who never left the land, and those who since had moved there and intermarried, these fifth-century-BCE Judeans are living together uncomfortably with competing messages as to what faithful living entails now (see, for example, Isa. 56:1–8; Ezra 9:1–2, 10–15; Neh. 5:1–5). Which of the rival leaders clamoring for power are they to follow? The Levitical purists? The Isaianic reconciliationists? The radical apocalypticists?

Malachi does not exactly take sides. Instead, he offers another possible direction, namely, to go back to the principles of the covenant so as to be rewarded (see Mal. 3:16–4:6). While sympathizing with the Levitical purists, the prophet upholds Moses as a model of righteousness and thus faithful living (Mal. 4:4). If those principles of the past are to be lived out in the present and future, then fundamental change may be possible. Even the possibility of the return of the prophet Elijah is promised. Though its details remain enigmatic, the result is a vision of intergenerational reconciliation (Mal. 4:5–6).

Analogies and allusions abound between the people addressed by Malachi and contemporary congregations in the United States. Competing voices proclaim the "right" direction; rival leaders clamor for power. What would constitute faithful covenant living during this season of Advent?

ANGELA BAUER-LEVESQUE

7. Pierre Briant, *From Cyrus to Alexander: A History of the Persian Empire* (Winona Lake, IN: Eisenbrauns, 1998).

HOMILETICAL PERSPECTIVE

The word of the Lord came to Malachi as a word of promise. That promise comes as good news to us; but there is also at least a degree of uneasiness in the promise. There are some elements of the promise that we would love to have fulfilled and other elements that we would just as soon leave unfulfilled.

This blend of joy and apprehension at the prospect of promise fulfillment is most clearly reflected in verse 2: "But who can endure the day of his coming, and who can stand when he appears? For he is like a refiner's fire and like fullers' soap." The believer responds to this promise by wondering exactly what is meant by the refining. What exactly in my life is in need of refining? And how much will it hurt? What might I have to give up (or what might be taken from me) before I would be refined like gold and silver?

In many ways, our response to this text is probably not that much different from the response of Malachi's original audience. Like them, we want to stand and see that day. We want our offerings to be pleasing to the Lord. We want to see the restoration of the covenant. We want to see things made right, the way God intended—and yet . . . and yet we are not so sure. We do not want to go through too much change or pain to see it happen.

This tension between joy and apprehension could provide great fodder for preaching, as we try to hear this promise anew and to reflect on our relationship to it. From a homiletical perspective, we ask how we can best approach the tension and gain some understanding. Two approaches lend themselves readily to addressing the tension in the promise of something new: we can reflect on the anticipation of a couple expecting a child, and we can reflect socially and culturally on what might really be changed when God's promised messenger of the covenant does come.

The culture of every people has stories about the anticipation involved in those nine months of waiting for a child to be born. Whether you retell a story from film or television or you tell your own story, the important point to make is that major events in life often come with very mixed emotions and mixed feelings. Even in the midst of joy at the prospect of this new life, this new person to love, there is often fear about the unknowns involved.

One story that reflects these ambivalences appears in the acclaimed 2007 film *Juno*. The title character in the film, a pregnant high-school student, wrestles throughout the movie, whose time frame is the nine-month pregnancy, with what this pregnancy and child mean for her relationship with friends, family, the baby's father, prospective adoptive parents, and herself. This story may help our parishioners reflect on our own feelings at hearing Malachi's promise. Juno wants to see this baby born and be healthy and have a good life. But what exactly does that mean for her? What does she have to sacrifice to get there? What will be changed in her life, regardless of the choices she makes going forward?

Another interesting layer of *Juno* for this text is the degree to which events are outside of Juno's control during the pregnancy. There are some choices she can make and some ways that she can affect outcomes, but there are many ways that she cannot. After hand-selecting adoptive parents for her as-yet unborn child, Juno comes to discover that nothing is guaranteed and people sometimes turn out to be different from what you at first may have thought. Events that have deep meaning for Juno and her child happen outside of her effective control. In the same way, God's promise of covenant restoration happens outside of our control. It is God's promise and God's restoration. It will happen, in God's way and whether we are ready for it or not.

Another approach to the same themes may come from some quite honest reflection on our church and our broader society. What might be refined and purified in God's promised refining fire? When God's promise, spoken through Malachi, is finally fulfilled, what will look different in our church? our world? our lives? A word of warning about this approach: this text is not an occasion to attack enemies or to point out all the things that some imagined "they" are doing wrong. Rather, *we* are the ones who are going to be refined. *We* are the ones in need of refining.

Look inside. Look inside yourself. Look inside your congregation. Look inside your church. What will God's refining look like? Perhaps the faces in our pews will reflect the rainbow of pigmentation in God's world more than they do. Perhaps there will be fewer luxury cars in the church parking lot and more beds for the homeless. What will our worship and our stewardship look like if "the offering of Judah and Jerusalem [and Chicago and Dallas and Tuscaloosa and Juneau and First Presbyterian and St. Martin's Lutheran] will be pleasing to the Lord" (v. 4)? These would be worthwhile questions to ponder.

In closing a sermon prepared with either of these approaches, it would be very helpful to emphasize that the promise of this restoration and refining is sure. It will happen, and it will happen under God's control and in God's time. The refining is not waiting for us to feel good about it. God's promise is sure, and it is good news. We will be re-formed in God's image, and it will be good. No matter how we feel about it now. No matter what we may be afraid of now. When we are refined and purified as God promises, it will be good.

SETH MOLAND-KOVASH

Matthew 24:36–44

THEOLOGICAL PERSPECTIVE

In contrast to some Eastern religions that view time as an endless cycle of birth, death, and rebirth, Christianity with its Judaic roots is a deeply historical religion. This history begins with God's creation of the world and ends with God's judgment and re-creation of it. Christians look backward, remembering God's mighty acts of salvation over the generations, and forward, anticipating the vindication of God's ways in a new heaven and a new earth. They live, as Karl Barth said, "between the times."

The season of Advent invites us to consider again the character of Christian existence "between the times." On the one hand, Advent reminds us of God's promises to Israel of Immanuel. God comes in human flesh to deliver God's people from sin and evil. On the other hand, Advent calls us to anticipate the day on which this Immanuel will return as King of kings and Lord of lords. He will put all that resists him, even death itself, under his feet. Living between the times, we give thanks to God for the Christ child, even as we plead with God to realize, once and for all, the kingdom that Jesus declared to be at hand.

Matthew 24:36–44 stands in a series of sayings and parables about a day of judgment that will inaugurate this kingdom to come. Jesus warns that this day will take the world by surprise. As in Noah's time, people will be going about their everyday business—eating and drinking, marrying and giving in marriage—with no awareness of God's impending judgment. They will be like a householder who fails to anticipate the hour at which the thief will break in. Not even the angels or the Son know the day or hour. The point is that we must be ready for the Lord at any time. When he finally appears, those who are ready will be saved, and those who are not ready will perish.

Jesus reiterates these themes in three parables in the following chapter (Matt. 25). The first tells of ten bridesmaids who wait for a bridegroom. When he finally arrives in the middle of the night, he receives the five who wisely kept oil in their lamps but shuts the door to the five who foolishly let theirs run out. The second tells of a master who, leaving on a long journey, entrusts his servants with his money. When he returns, he commends two servants who made wise investments, but condemns the one who only buried his portion in the ground. The third parable, like the first two, warns of a day of judgment that will divide humanity into two groups. Those ("the sheep") who fed and clothed "the least of these" also fed and clothed the Lord, though they knew it not; those ("the goats") who failed to feed and clothe them failed to feed and clothe the Lord, though they too knew it not. All three parables explicate the point in Matthew 24:44: "Therefore you also must be ready, for the Son of Man is coming at an unexpected hour."

Christians have long debated when and how this day of judgment will take place. One line of thinking has combined Matthew 24:36–44 with other apocalyptic passages in the Hebrew Bible and New Testament to work out a time line of events that are already underway or soon to transpire. Representative of this position is Hal Lindsey's *The Late, Great Planet Earth* (a bestseller in the 1970s) or more recently Tim LaHaye and Jerry Jenkins's *Left Behind* novels. Like other American fundamentalists, these authors anticipate a day on which God's elect will be raptured—that is, lifted up in their physical bodies to the Lord—while the reprobate are "left behind" to incur God's wrath. We must get ready, because these things may take place yet in our lifetime.

A second line of thinking has seen the day of judgment not at the end of human history but at the time of each individual's death. Each of us will stand before God's judgment seat as soon as we have taken our last breath. We will have to give an accounting of our life and be weighed in the Lord's balance. Again, the lesson is clear: we dare not put off doing what Jesus has commanded. None of us can know when death will overtake us, and then it will be too late.

A third understanding of this passage emphasizes the symbolic character of Jesus' language. The point is not to speculate about a day of judgment sometime in the future, whether at the end of all humanity or at the death of each individual, but rather to confront us with God's radical claims on us here and now. Each day is a day of judgment, so I should always be asking myself, Am I living in the way of Christ? Am I trusting in him alone? Have I allowed myself to be distracted by selfish cares?

Other Christians have combined aspects of these positions, or have developed variations on them. None of these interpretations will be true to the gospel, however, unless they keep the day of judgment firmly in relationship to the new day that has already dawned in the life, death, and resurrection of Jesus Christ. We live between the times! A theology of the coming kingdom is most faithful to the biblical witness when it reminds us that the Christ who judges us is also the Christ who endured judgment for our sake; that God's judgment never contradicts or overrides God's grace; and that the readiness to which Jesus calls us is shaped not by fear of the future, but rather by gratitude for life in the kingdom that Christ already offers us.

To live between the times is, above all, to trust and hope that God has begun, and will continue, to transform us more and more into the stature of

Christ, in whom all of God's mercy and loving-kindness becomes manifest. Advent calls us into a continuing history of relationship with the Christ who meets us whichever way we turn, whether toward the past, the present, or the future.

JOHN P. BURGESS

PASTORAL PERSPECTIVE

The advent of Advent with its emphasis on the coming of the Son of Man produces two quite different reactions among congregants.

Some Christians think that the whole emphasis on Christ's Parousia (i.e., appearing) is much ado about nothing, or at least much ado about nothing believable. If they are faithful churchgoers, they endure the annual Advent apocalyptic texts and look forward to next week, when John the Baptist, that tangible historical figure, helps us look forward to Jesus.

Some Christians think that Christ's second coming is the heart of the gospel. As Karl Barth is supposed to have enjoined, they start the day with the Bible in one hand and the newspaper in the other, but their hermeneutical strategy is often quite different from Barth's. They search the Bible for signs of the end times, and they search the newspaper to see if those signs are yet in view.

Those Christians who are agnostic about last things are tempted to fall into a state of perpetual apathy. Those Christians who are focused on last things are tempted to fall into a state of perpetual anxiety. Our passage encourages faith rather than apathy and hope rather than anxiety.

The Advent Community of Faith. The passage from Matthew calls us away from historical apathy. I once heard the distinguished New Testament scholar and bishop Krister Stendahl say that we misread our congregations if we think they are most often puzzling about the eternal life of each individual. On the contrary, said Stendahl, contemporary Christians are most often puzzling about whether history has any significance.

The passage from Matthew reminds us of the profound biblical faith that God is sovereign over all of human history. However metaphorically, however mythologically, Jesus tells us in this discourse that the God who created history at the beginning is not only history's goad but history's goal.

Pastoral attention to the themes of Advent requires a major counterproposal to Macbeth's cynical apathy: "Life is a tale told by an idiot, full of sound and fury, signifying nothing."[8] For the Bible and for the church, life is a tale told by a strong and sovereign God, enacted according to God's pleasure. It

---

8. William Shakespeare, *Macbeth*, act 5, scene 5.

is full of both judgment and grace, and it moves toward the time when God will make all things new.

For Advent especially we attend to liturgy, music, pastoral care, and Christian education that help assure God's people that we *are* God's people, and that the history in which we live is God's story, moving from God to God.

The Advent Community of Hope. Today's passage calls us away from historical anxiety. Of course it is full of signs of the end, but the initial warning steers us away from the temptation to keep apocalyptic calendars on the kitchen wall: "But about that day and hour no one knows, neither the angels of heaven, nor the Son, but only the Father" (v. 36). The serenity prayer, usually attributed to Reinhold Niebuhr, asks us to accept the things that we cannot change. Sometimes it is even harder to acknowledge the facts that we cannot know; yet with that acceptance can come a kind of eschatologically sensitive serenity. If Jesus is hopeful as he waits for a consummation he himself does not fully understand, surely we can learn our hope from him.

In pastoral care and in religious formation, one of the gifts we most desire is for people to be able to trust in the future without controlling or even knowing the details of what is yet to come. All our hope is founded in God.

The Advent Community of Memory. Today's passage helps us look forward without apathy or anxiety because it is not afraid to look back. What this particular passage looks back on is the time of Noah. The tale is a cautionary reminder that we ignore the judgment and power of God at great cost. The tale is also a helpful reminder that sometimes by looking back at what God has done we can have confidence in what God will do, in God's own time.

Part of the power of Scripture is that it provides the stories that are foreshadowings (not blueprints) for what God is doing in our own time and will do. Part of the power of community is that we can look back together at the moments in our past where God was present to chasten and to bless, and find there hope and admonition for the future.

Liturgy is the great remembering. Surrounding the sermon are the hymns and prayers and readings that recall what God has done for God's people and for God's world. It is bad faith to come to Advent services as if we had no idea that God has come to us in Jesus Christ. We wait in hope because we wait in memory.

While pastoral care is by no means confined to pastoral psychology, we have learned over these past decades that looking back can be essential to moving ahead. Think about Noah, we say to the parishioner. Think about the stories in your own life that showed forth the judgment and the promises of God. Move forward in that light.

The Advent Community of Alertness. One major function of our apocalyptic text is to remind us to keep awake. Faith, hope, and memory all help draw us toward Christian responsibility. We respond to the God who acted in Jesus Christ, who acts now, and who will act in the consummation of history.

As the next chapter of Matthew's Gospel will make abundantly clear, we also keep awake to the needs of others (see Matt. 25:31–46). One day Jesus may appear in the clouds, suddenly, like a thief in the night. But before that—as Matthew reminds us—Jesus will appear just around the corner, suddenly, like a hungry person, or a neighbor ill-clothed, or someone sick or imprisoned.

"Therefore [we] also must be ready" (v. 44).

DAVID L. BARTLETT

EXEGETICAL PERSPECTIVE

The season of Advent usually begins with an eschatological text, as a way of framing Advent as the end of an old order and the birth of a new era. Matthew's eschatological text can be outlined as follows:

24:36	theme: watchfulness amid uncertainty
24:37–39	illustration of theme (days of Noah)
24:40–41	two further illustrations of the theme (men and women)
24:42	repetition of theme frames parable (application 1)
24:43	parable as illustration of theme
24:44	repetition of theme frames parable (application 2)

The passage we are studying comes from Matthew's fifth discourse, which deals with eschatological matters and judgment (Matt. 24:1–25:46).

The theme of this section of Matthew's discourse is the necessity for watchfulness in light of the uncertainty surrounding the coming (Parousia) of Jesus. Verse 36 makes a startling claim: "neither the angels of heaven nor the Son" know when "that day" will occur. It is remarkable how many interpreters seem to believe that they can accomplish what the Son confesses he cannot do. This view of the limit of the Son's knowledge is entirely compatible with passages like the *kenōsis* hymn in Philippians 2:5–11, so the statement should not surprise us so much as it may induce a certain humility into our efforts to discern God's will.

Three examples follow in verses 37–39, 40–41. The first (vv. 37–39) draws on the days of Noah. The figure of Noah has been variously interpreted in biblical traditions. In Hebrews 11:7, Noah heeds God's warning of impending catastrophic judgment and so builds an ark that saves his family, but his faith condemns the world. In 1 Peter 3:20, Noah's rescuing his family from the flood serves as a metaphor for baptism that saves us through water. In 2 Peter 2:5, the writer notes that God did not spare the world from judgment but saved Noah, "a herald of righteousness." The prophet Ezekiel groups Noah together with Daniel and Job to indicate that God's judgment is so great that even their presence would save themselves but no one else (14:14, 20). Finally, Isaiah speaks of "the days of Noah" (54:9) to reaffirm the covenant with Jerusalem.

The saying about the days of Noah in our Advent passage belongs to Q (Luke 17:26–36 // Matt. 24:36–44). What makes this saying so unusual is that it focuses on those who failed to prepare themselves, not on the righteousness of Noah. The "herald of righteousness" fades into the background, and the heedless and thoughtless step onto center stage. The point of the sayings is to emphasize that people were just doing business as usual while the specter of judgment hung over their heads unnoticed. "Eating and drinking" do not refer to drunkenness and gluttony, just everyday meals, and "marrying and giving in marriage" indicate that people presumed that there would be a future, assuming there was time for another generation to be born. Then all this came crashing down upon them, and they were swept away.

The next two illustrations make a similar point but indicate the two-sided nature of judgment, namely, that some are saved and others are not. The universality of judgment is indicated by the fact that the first two are men, and the second pair are women. In each case, they are involved in gender-specific behavior in Jesus' culture. The men are in a field, and the women are in the courtyard shared by several houses using a common grinding wheel. Both are well-chosen illustrations to indicate the extent of judgment and its invasion of domestic space and fields alike. In both instances, the figures are engaged in their normal, everyday activities.

This reading raises an interesting and sometimes overlooked question. Is the one taken being saved or being snatched up for judgment? What is the fate of the one left behind? Based on the use of the two verbs (taken=*paralambanō* and left=*aphiēmi*) in Matthew, it would appear that the one taken is the fortunate and watchful disciple who remains undistracted by the signs of the times enumerated in Matthew 24:3–28. In the birth narrative, the verb "taken" is used four times (2:13, 14, 20, 21) to indicate taking the child to safety. In 20:17 and 26:37, Jesus "takes" the disciples aside. In the "days of Noah" saying, those who are taken in the ark are saved while those who are left perish. So, in Matthew's vocabulary, "taken" (*paralam-banō*) seems to refer to being redeemed from danger, while being left behind (*aphiēmi*) carries the sense of being forsaken or abandoned.

The "days of Noah" illustration and the paired scenes of judgment share a common theme. Because the day of the "Son of Man" will come unexpectedly and cannot be anticipated, one must develop the art of watchful living. Daily work in the field and in the courtyard is necessary to maintain life, but one must always peer through the ordinary days to discern the coming of that extraordinary day. However, one is not to waste time on wild speculations over the claims of false messiahs (24:3–14). The coming judgment will separate the redeemed from the lost.

The parable of the Thief in the Night (v. 43) is surrounded by two applications (vv. 42, 44), both of which make the same point. However, the surprising depiction of the coming of the Son of Man as a thief raises a question. To whom might the reign of heaven and the coming Son of Man be seen as a threat? Whose hegemony would be undermined? Which "strong man's house" would be "plunder[ed of] his property" (12:28–29)?

Amos could say to an Israel eagerly anticipating the coming day of the Lord, "Why do you want the day of the LORD? It is darkness, not light" (Amos 5:18–20). Jesus' comments here may indicate that he shares a view of the Day of the Lord much like Amos's. The master of the house is simply the negative counterpart of the watchful disciple. For what is the disciple being watchful?

A new advent!

WILLIAM R. HERZOG II

HOMILETICAL PERSPECTIVE

Upon noticing the Gospel reading assigned for this Sunday, more than one preacher may wince, if not grimace with pain. That facial expression is an outward and visible sign of an inward and spiritual struggle between going where a text wants to go and staying where the people think they want to be.

Typically, the Advent congregation already has Christmas on its mind and is tilting toward December 25. Hanging the greens, decking the halls, and already caroling Christmas seem high on the list of congregational expectations.

This Gospel reading is at odds with this congregational expectation because it tilts toward a different day altogether. Matthew and the Jesus he presents seem not at all interested in Christmas, but are focused instead on an apocalyptic day in the unknown future, when the Son of Man will suddenly return and lives will be suddenly and surprisingly changed. This "shall come again" language of Scripture and the Apostles' Creed are enough to give more than a few of our people the creeps, and many would prefer that it be "left behind." One need not lean very far to the theological left to be prone to dismiss this line of thinking as somewhere way out there to the right.

When, then, the preacher sits down in the study with this lection, there is both the powerful push toward Christmas and the equally powerful pull away from apocalyptic eschatology. Still, in spite of this push and pull, there is the press of the text, just as powerful and commanding.

If the preacher lets the text win in this push, pull, and press, the initial wince can open into the soft smile of a growing insight. The insight comes when one is suddenly taken by the idea that there is no reason why the first part of this text should not be taken literally. While the text may tilt toward a mysterious future day, it actually remains firmly put in an ordinary present day. This present day is characterized by uncertainty, by a perplexity that extends all the way to the angels and even to the Son. Since we know we are confused much of the time, there is ample reason and evidence to take this part of the text literally. If we begin here, our people might stop pushing toward Christmas and pulling away from apocalypticism, and start listening to a sermon about today.

Most people know they are perplexed. They also know they want to be persons of faith. Along with all the problems associated with their perplexity is the problem posed by the spoken or unspoken assumption that persons with real faith are not perplexed but clear. Instead, the faith of our listeners does not bring everything into focus. What God would have them do in regard to their daily decisions—much less their daunting difficulties—is far from certain. They have neither chapter nor verse nor the foggiest notion how to figure these deep matters through.

Since many of them, like many of us, are good at guilt, they assume they are baffled because they are at fault, because their faith is flawed and weak. Our text presents a splendid opportunity to show them that uncertainty is a condition of even the best biblical faith. This does not solve any of the unanswered questions, of course, but it may begin to bring our people a kind of rapture of relief because it takes the pressure off. It is a relief to know Christ does not expect us to know everything.

We are not expected to know everything, but we are expected to do something. The Jesus of the verses before us calls persons to a life of work in a spirit of wakefulness. Work in this sense means activity here and now. Biblical faith as Jesus envisions it is not so concerned with otherworldly matters that it neglects this world's affairs. Matthew's Jesus has an eye on what is to come and believes something decisive is going to happen in the future, but he keeps attention focused on the present day and the needs of the hour. We find this in the manner in which he directs people to the field, the mill, the daily grind, the ordinary places of human endeavor where life is lived. This region of the mundane is where faithfulness happens, and it is not to be neglected. Biblical faith knows it does not know everything, but it does know it is called to do something here and now. Whatever else Christians may be, they are a workforce in the world.

The work the Christian does is to be accomplished in a spirit of wakefulness or watchfulness. The key element for Jesus is not the work, important as it is. The indispensable part of faithful work is the awareness or sensitivity Jesus names as watchfulness or wakefulness. He does not define this awareness with clarity, spelling out its details—more uncertainty!—but indications are it at least means that work is not all there is. Work will not do everything and cannot do everything. Hope will come—the deepest, best, and highest shall come—not from our work but from somewhere outside and beyond it.

So the sermon has brought another moment of rapture, has it not? If the first rapture of relief came when the people were taken up by the idea that they need not know everything, the second comes when they are taken up by the idea that they need not do everything—to work their or anyone else's salvation. The voice of Jesus has assured them: if they do what they can in a spirit of hope and trust, they will do enough.

MARK E. YURS

Third Sunday of Advent

[14]Sing aloud, O daughter Zion;
    shout, O Israel!
Rejoice and exult with all your heart,
    O daughter Jerusalem!
[15]The LORD has taken away the judgments against you,
    he has turned away your enemies.
The king of Israel, the LORD, is in your midst;
    you shall fear disaster no more.
[16]On that day it shall be said to Jerusalem:
Do not fear, O Zion;
    do not let your hands grow weak.
[17]The LORD, your God, is in your midst,
    a warrior who gives victory;
he will rejoice over you with gladness,
    he will renew you in his love;
he will exult over you with loud singing
    [18]as on a day of festival.
I will remove disaster from you,
    so that you will not bear reproach for it.
[19]I will deal with all your oppressors
    at that time.
And I will save the lame
    and gather the outcast,
and I will change their shame into praise
    and renown in all the earth.
[20]At that time I will bring you home,
    at the time when I gather you;
for I will make you renowned and praised
    among all the peoples of the earth,
when I restore your fortunes
    before your eyes, says the LORD.

²⁴"But in those days, after that suffering,
  the sun will be darkened,
    and the moon will not give its light,
²⁵and the stars will be falling from heaven,
    and the powers in the heavens will be shaken.

²⁶Then they will see 'the Son of Man coming in clouds' with great power and glory. ²⁷Then he will send out the angels, and gather his elect from the four winds, from the ends of the earth to the ends of heaven.

²⁸"From the fig tree learn its lesson: as soon as its branch becomes tender and puts forth its leaves, you know that summer is near. ²⁹So also, when you see these things taking place, you know that he is near, at the very gates. ³⁰Truly I tell you, this generation will not pass away until all these things have taken place. ³¹Heaven and earth will pass away, but my words will not pass away.

³²"But about that day or hour no one knows, neither the angels in heaven, nor the Son, but only the Father. ³³Beware, keep alert; for you do not know when the time will come. ³⁴It is like a man going on a journey, when he leaves home and puts his slaves in charge, each with his work, and commands the doorkeeper to be on the watch. ³⁵Therefore, keep awake—for you do not know when the master of the house will come, in the evening, or at midnight, or at cockcrow, or at dawn, ³⁶or else he may find you asleep when he comes suddenly. ³⁷And what I say to you I say to all: Keep awake."

ORDER OF WORSHIP

OPENING WORDS / CALL TO WORSHIP

There will be signs in the heavens   *Mark 13:24-27*
and distress among the nations.
When Christ returns in power and glory
people will faint with fear.
But when you see these things, lift up your heads:
our redemption is drawing near!
Heaven and earth may pass away,   *Mark 13:31*
but the Word of God will stand unshaken.

LIGHTING OF THE ADVENT CANDLES

[Reader 1]: We light this candle as a symbol of
God's love for us and our love for one another.

[Reader 2]: For the Lord rejoices over us with gladness,
and renews us in his love. He exults over us
with singing and turns our shame to praise.

[All]: **Come, Lord Jesus, come!**

HYMN, SPIRITUAL, OR PSALM

CALL TO CONFESSION

Assured that God hears our repentance,
let us turn our minds to the truth,
confessing our sins to God and one another.

PRAYER OF CONFESSION

The Lord is near.
In your presence, Holy God,
we confess that we need repentance.
We have broken your commands against idolatry.
We do not live in peace with your creation or your people.
We have not trusted your word, and we are afraid.
Forgive us, restore us, and turn our shame into praise,
for the sake of the One who proclaims the good news
and for the sake of all the world. Amen.

DECLARATION OF FORGIVENESS

In the name of the one God
who lives and moves among us,
you are forgiven.
The Lord has taken away the judgments against you.   *Zeph. 3:15*
Do not worry. Live in peace.

PRAYER OF THE DAY

Merciful God,
you come into our midst
longing for communion with us,
becoming one of us.
Break our resistance to life with you,
show us the path toward just relations,

and bring us into your unimaginable peace;
in Jesus' name. **Amen.**

HYMN, SPIRITUAL, OR PSALM

PRAYER FOR ILLUMINATION

God of signs and wonders,   *Mark 13:24–37*
we come to your word again and again,
seeking understanding
and the new life it offers.
By the power of your Holy Spirit,
illumine our hearts and minds
so that we may believe this testimony
and have eternal life.
In the name of Jesus Christ,
our teacher and Savior, we pray. **Amen.**

SCRIPTURE READINGS

SERMON

HYMN, SPIRITUAL, OR PSALM

PRAYERS OF INTERCESSION

God our Helper,
we thank you for keeping our lives
always in your care and protection
and pray for any and all who are in harm's way.
For those walking in the midst of danger . . .
for those who are treading a slippery path . . .
for those exhausted and seeking relief . . .
for those who face a mountain of worry or debt
or any other obstacles . . .
Be Guardian and Guide, we pray,
setting all our feet on your paths of righteousness and peace.
We pray for those who are struggling
with a new challenge or call . . .
with a major transition in life or livelihood . . .
with their faith and understanding . . .
with grief, ancient or new . . .

Keep in your tender care and mercy, O God,
those who are sick in mind, body, or spirit . . .
those weighed down by depression or pain . . .
those recuperating from surgery or accident. . . .
Protect not only us and those we love,
but also the whole wide world you so love.
In places of war, bring peace . . .
in places beset by natural disaster, bring calm
and restoration . . .
where there is unrest and injustice, make justice our aim.
Where hope has grown tired and thin, lift our sights,
so that we may see hope beyond hope,
life beyond death,
and you, lifted up before us.
In the name of Christ,
who gave himself for our sake, we pray. **Amen.**

LORD'S PRAYER

INVITATION TO THE OFFERING
Let us bring to God our offerings,
with thanksgiving that God provides more than
enough for all.
Let us give, as each is able, for the benefit of Christ's
church and God's world.

PRAYER OF THANKSGIVING/DEDICATION
Gracious God, in gratitude for all that you have given us,
we bring our tithes, offerings, and labor
to help feed a world hungry for healing and hope;
for the sake of Jesus Christ. **Amen.**

HYMN, SPIRITUAL, OR PSALM

CHARGE
Fear not, people of the Lord.   *Zeph. 3:15–17*
God brings you strength and victory.

As you depart this day,   *Zeph. 3:17*
may you feel the Lord's presence
and hear his song singing over you
now and forevermore.

SONG SUGGESTIONS

"Come Down, O Love Divine" (*ELW* 804, *GC* 465, *GTG* 282, *TNCH* 289, *UMH* 475)

"For You, O Lord, My Soul in Stillness Waits" (*GC* 328, *GTG* 89)

"Heaven Is Singing for Joy" (*ELW* 664, *GTG* 382)

"Lift Up Your Heads, Ye Mighty Gates" (*CH* 129, *GTG* 93, *TNCH* 117, *UMH* 213)

"Light One Candle to Watch for Messiah," stanza 3 (*ELW* 240, *GTG* 85)

"Lo, He Comes with Clouds Descending" (*EH* 57, *ELW* 435, *GTG* 348, *UMH* 718)

"Now the Heavens Start to Whisper" (*GTG* 94)

"Wake, Awake, for Night Is Flying" (*ELW* 436, *UMH* 720)

CHILDREN'S SERMON

Based on Mark 13:28–29

Let me tell you a story about a very cold winter, the iciest winter ever. It was so cold that the lakes and roads and ground stayed frozen all winter long. You could not climb a tree because it was so icy that you would slide right back down! And the ground was frozen so solid that a dog could not even dig a hole to bury its bone! The air was so cold you would not want to play outside very long, because your nose and ears would freeze and you would not be able to feel your toes!

There was an old man who stayed in his house all that winter. It was too cold to go outside and sit on the bench under his favorite apple tree. He had to bundle up in sweaters and wool socks to keep warm, and it got dark so early that he just went to bed right after dinner. It was really boring, and he got so sad as the weeks went on, through December and January and February. He wanted to be able to go outside again, and sit under his favorite apple tree, and grow flowers and vegetables in his garden. But day after day, he would look out his window and see the ice all over every branch of his favorite apple tree, and he knew it was still winter.

One morning, when he woke up in his bed, all covered in heavy blankets and his warm flannel pajamas, he heard a drip, drip, drip coming from outside. He got out of bed and ran to the window to see what was making that dripping sound. And do you know what it was? It was the ice on his favorite apple tree, melting and drip, drip, dripping onto the bench below.

But was it still winter? he wondered. He put his hand on the glass of the window, and it still felt cold. It must still be winter, he thought. Every day, he looked out the window to see if it was still winter. The ice was gone from his favorite apple tree, but the window still felt cold, so he stayed inside.

Finally, one day he looked out the window, and before he could even put his hand to the glass to see if it still felt cold, he saw something on his favorite apple tree: tiny green buds! Leaves were starting to sprout! Spring was finally here!

Jesus told a story kind of like this one to let people know that even when things seem dark and maybe kind of scary, you can watch for signs of light and hope, and know that Jesus is here.

Prayer: Thank you, God, for the signs of life you send us all year round. Amen.

SERMON HELPS

Zephaniah 3:14–20

THEOLOGICAL PERSPECTIVE

As Christians travel ever further in the journey of anticipation that is Advent, the prophets continue to yield important insights into the meaning of the season, and the character and fulfillment of God's promises.[1] This week's lection from the prophet Zephaniah carries within it the communal memory of suffering and divine judgment, yet anticipates fulfillment of God's promises. Prominent theological themes in this text include (1) God's exaltation of the suffering and the outcast and (2) incarnation.

---

1. Although it is commonly agreed that this text was written during the continued Assyrian domination in Jerusalem, the prophet invites his hearers to gather for praise in anticipation of coming restoration. See Marvin A. Sweeney, *Zephaniah: A Commentary*, Hermeneia (Minneapolis: Fortress Press, 2003), 193–208.

God's Exaltation of the Suffering and the Outcast. Zephaniah is acutely aware of the corruption and injustice perpetrated by Judah's leaders. Right up to the admonition to "wait" in 3:8, Zephaniah details the spiritual and political oppression perpetrated by the leaders in Judah, and God's impending punishment: destruction. As a result of the social injustice, the oppressed are fearful and ashamed, while the powerful are haughty and corrupt and reject divine correction. While the prophet recounts all the ways in which God will deal with the oppressors, he reserves a special word for those who have suffered at their unjust hands: "I will deal with all your oppressors at that time. And I will save the lame and gather the outcast, and I will change their shame into praise and renown in all the earth" (3:19). In reading this text during Advent, we anticipate the Gospel reading for the fourth week, in which Mary sings praises unto God, who lifts up the lowly and brings down the powerful (Luke 1:46–55). The same themes are echoed, also, in Revelation 21:4: "mourning and crying and pain will be no more." In these two texts, as in the lectionary text for today, the relationship between the season of Advent and the advent of the kingdom of God start to become clear. God's promises have about them a preference for protecting and lifting up the lowly, the suffering, and the oppressed. We find an unfolding of God's promises in many places throughout the biblical narratives: in the prophetic word, in the coming of Jesus, and in God's alternative future, the kingdom of God. Jürgen Moltmann defined this as the essence of theological hope: "biblical thought always understands hope as the expectation of a good future which rests on God's promise."[2] Of course, readers should not move too quickly to associate Zephaniah's words with either the birth of Jesus or an eschatological future. At the same time, however, as the Christian celebration of the birth of Jesus nears, readers are challenged to remember the character of God's continuing and living promise to protect and exalt the lowly. This is the context in which the prophetic word, the coming of the Messiah, and the shape of the kingdom of God derive their meaning. It also is the context in which the character of God is revealed.

It is important to note, however, that Zephaniah's praise of the humble ought not be interpreted solely as a universal valorization of self-effacing humility. Rather, the prophetic word affirms that God's purposes are to make right systems of injustice, to heal the shame that results from oppression. In the exaltation of the humble and lowly, Zephaniah finds both a divine rejection of the abuses of power and a divine promise to protect the weak and the outcast.

2. Jürgen Moltmann, "Hope," in *The Westminster Dictionary of Christian Theology*, ed. Alan Richardson and John Stephen Bowden (Philadelphia: Westminster Press, 1983), 271.

Incarnation. Twice in this text (vv. 15, 17) the prophet affirms God's presence with the people, affirming that God is and will continue to be in their midst. God's presence does two things in these verses: it protects and it rejoices. The people will live without fear, trusting that God saves them from disaster and enemy attack. God's presence does more than remove threats, however. God's presence among the people is animating, in that God rejoices with them, renews them, and exults over them. God frees and strengthens the people by being present among them, such that their hands should not "grow weak." John Calvin interpreted the prophet's words in this way: "And it is what we also know by experience, that when fear prevails in our hearts we are as it were lifeless, so that we cannot raise even a finger to do anything: but when hope animates us, there is a vigor in the whole body, so that alacrity appears everywhere."[3] God's living among the people releases them from fear and shame, invigorating them to work for the good.

God's promises to those who suffer are not effected from a divine distance, but by God's very presence among the people. God comes to humanity in flesh, most assuredly. The Advent season walks us forward toward that birth the angels sang. But Zephaniah assures us that God also comes to humanity in the community of faith. God's presence heals, enlivens, and challenges humanity to lean into God's promises for an alternative future. As the United Presbyterian Church affirmed in the Confession of 1967, "Already God's reign is present as a ferment in the world, stirring hope in (women and men)." In dwelling among the people, God nourishes and makes real the promised future of peace and joy that theological hope imagines. This is a strong and hopeful message that will hearten the faithful on this Third Sunday of Advent.

JENNIFER RYAN AYRES

PASTORAL PERSPECTIVE

"Thank God we can't know the future, or we'd never get out of bed." Playwright Tracey Letts scripts an unhappy adult daughter to pass along the family pessimism to her own daughter. *August: Osage County* is a Pulitzer Prize– and Tony Award–winning play and film about a family convened on the occasion of the father's funeral. Some families rise to the occasion of good behavior during a crisis. This one sinks even deeper in dysfunction. The alcoholic father has committed suicide; the pill-addicted widow-mother is mean and manipulative. One of the daughters who seems happy and

---

3. John Calvin, *Commentaries on the Twelve Minor Prophets,* vol. 4, ed. and trans. John Owen (Grand Rapids: Eerdmans, 1950), 303.

healthy is revealed to be in love with her cousin, who is revealed to be her half brother; another is trying to hide a marital separation, and another is about to marry a pedophile. The granddaughter is stoned and promiscuous. They all smoke something and drink too much and swear excessively. All of that is the context of the disturbing and riveting line: "Thank God we can't know the future, or we'd never get out of bed." The playwright reflects a pervasive, corrosive milieu of fear and grim resignation in our time. In his time, the prophet Zephaniah rehearsed a similar drama of human sin, involving "violence and fraud" (1:9), arrogance, and immorality that produced disaster, reproach, and shame. But, thank God, Zephaniah knows something of God's future.

In Advent you may preach or read from Malachi, Jeremiah, Zephaniah, Isaiah, or Micah. The prophet is as much the voice of Advent as is the evangelist. Why? Prophets say what no one wants to hear, what no one wants to believe. Prophets point in directions no one wants to look. They hear God when everybody else has concluded God is silent. They see God where nobody else would guess that God is present. They feel God. Prophets feel God's compassion for us, God's anger with us, God's joy in us. They dream God's dreams and utter wake-up calls; they hope God's hopes and announce a new future; they will God's will and live it against all odds. Prophets sing God's song and sometimes interrupt the program with a change of tune.

Zephaniah's song calls people to lament and repent. Jerusalem is idolatrous and complacent; the nations are corrupt. God is indignant. Today's text needs to be heard in its context in order to capture the abrupt shift in the joyful imperative, "Sing aloud. . . . Rejoice and exult!" God's promised salvation interrupts a tirade of judgment with a song of joy. The "day of darkness and gloom" (1:15) is supplanted by a day of gladness.

Zephaniah, thank God, knows the future and wants us to get up and rejoice! The future will be different from the present and even different from the future that had been foreseen. There will be no disaster, no reproach, no shame, no fear. Why do we listen to the prophets during Advent? Because centuries before the birth of Jesus Christ they were messengers of essential good news: "Do not fear. . . . The LORD, your God, is in your midst." The prophet teaches the evangelist a basic phrase in the language of God, and again the prophetic word is a pastoral word, spoken into the heart of human experience.

"Do not fear" is not a plea, but a declaration. Luke speaks it to instill confidence in unsuspecting recipients of God's news: "Do not be afraid, Zechariah," "Do not be afraid, Mary." Later in the story we will hear, "Do not be afraid . . . I am bringing you good news of great joy." Another Gospel proclaims at its end, "Do not be afraid. . . . He is not here, for he has been raised" (Matt. 28:5–6).

"Do not fear" is repeated over and over again in these texts because human beings are afraid of many things. Read between the lines that follow in verses 16–20, and we read our own souls: We fear that God is not in our midst and that the enemies of good and God are winning. We fear that our hands are weak and powerless, atrophied by lack of useful work and helpful use, exercised in holding on but needing both physical and spiritual therapy to reach out. We fear insignificance, doubting that we matter in the course of events and dreading that we will be crushed by them. We fear political defeat and natural disaster. We fear shame and reproach, that our faults and foibles will be discovered and render us less than the person we had fooled ourselves and others into thinking we were. We are afraid that we won't have enough, won't be enough. We even fear that God may keep God's promises, and interrupt the safety of our fears and the familiarity of our enemies with something new. Zephaniah's pastoral word to the people of God acknowledges our fear and dispels it with a promise of a transforming joy and not a threat of judgment.

This text illumines the liturgical practice of lighting a rose-colored candle on the Advent wreath on the Third Sunday of Advent. Congregations that continue the liturgical color of purple for this season, rather than blue, have a visual symbol for an interjection of joy. Purple candles recall a time when Advent paralleled Lent as a season of penitence and was marked by practices of prayer and fasting. But on the Third Sunday a rose candle was lighted to symbolize joy, and the penitential fast was lifted. The Third Sunday of Advent is traditionally called Gaudete Sunday, from the Latin imperative, "Rejoice!" The name sounds the note of the epistle often read on this day, in which Paul enjoins the Philippians, "Rejoice in the Lord always; again I will say, Rejoice. . . . The Lord is near" (Phil. 4:4–5).

We are not a people who welcome interruptions. Zephaniah reminds us that through prophetic interruptions God offers us glimpses of a hopeful future that goes beyond getting us up in the morning. It frees us from fear and moves us to rejoice.

DEBORAH A. BLOCK

EXEGETICAL PERSPECTIVE

The short biblical book of Zephaniah locates itself in the seventh century BCE during the reign of King Josiah of Judah (640–609 BCE), who elsewhere in the Bible, namely, in the books of Kings and Chronicles, is characterized as the last great king, whose only equal was the great King David.

Zephaniah, however, witnesses another reality in the streets of Jerusalem. Lamenting idolatry, corruption, and injustice, the prophetic message found in the book of Zephaniah is constructed in a way that sets the stage for the Josianic reform of 621 BCE, a major movement to reintroduce the statutes and ordinances of the Sinai covenant (see the Deuteronomic Code in Deut. 12–26). The identity of the prophet remains unclear, even though the superscription of the book traces his roots back four generations (Zeph. 1:1), which is unusual for biblical prophets.[4] The fact that his father's name is Cushi has made some scholars wonder about a possible Ethiopian heritage of this prophet. The matter is complicated by royal Israelite heritage invoked in King Hezekiah. In any case, the need for legitimization of Zephaniah the prophet appears strong, be it for the color of his skin in a place of power or for the content of his message.

The book of Zephaniah consists predominantly of judgment oracles (eight out of nine in the book) invoking the day of the Lord (*yom YHWH*) (Zeph. 1:2–3:8), a special day when all will be judged and found in breach of the covenant. Indeed, the prophet Zephaniah announces cosmic destruction (1:2–3; 3:8), which includes particular attention to the people of Judah and Jerusalem, singling out the priesthood as particularly sinful and idolatrous (1:4). The language, reminiscent of the book of Isaiah (see Isa. 1:21–31; 2:5–22; 10:1–4; 28:1–13; etc.), has led some scholars to suggest that Zephaniah was a student of Isaiah of Jerusalem. Others have ascribed the Isaianic echoes to a postexilic editor. The fact that the prophet denounces Israel's sin as pride and puts his hope in a faithful remnant also fits well into an Isaianic tradition. The short book ends in a ninth oracle, an oracle of salvation for this very remnant, and those eschatological verses make up this reading for the Third Sunday of Advent.

Zephaniah 3:14–20 opens with an exhortation to daughter Zion and to Israel to sing. Addressed with female appellations, the people are to rejoice wholeheartedly (v. 14). The subsequent hymn belongs to the song tradition of women in the Hebrew Bible.[5] It especially echoes women's songs in times of crisis and celebration in other prophetic books (see, for example, Jer. 9:17–22; 31:2–6). The promises picture God having reversed judgment and reclaimed the throne (v. 15). As in the time before the institution of the monarchy, in these eschatological times there is no need for a human king. Indeed, accepting God as king reverts to the arrangements of the Sinai

---

4. See for example, Mária Eszenyei Széles, *Wrath and Mercy: A Commentary on the Books of Habakkuk and Zephaniah*, trans. George A. F. Knight (Grand Rapids: Eerdmans, 1987).
5. Carol L. Meyers, "Of Drums and Damsels: Women's Performance in Ancient Israel," *Biblical Archeologist* 54 (1991): 16–27.

covenant (see Exod. 19:1–6), the kind of relationship between God and people that the Josianic reform will favor. As a consequence, Jerusalem is admonished to fear no longer, because God will not only bring victory over the enemy but also join in rejoicing and song (vv. 16–17). Indeed, God will join together with the people in singing this hymn of praise.

Part of this promise is what the NRSV renders "he will renew you in his love"; the NIV reads "he will quiet you with his love"; and the Tanakh translation says, "He will soothe with His love" (v. 17b). While the NRSV gets its translation from the wording in the Septuagint, the other two translations mentioned try to render the corrupted Masoretic text with a possible emendation. Both concepts—the earlier one of the promise of God's love calming the people and the later one of God renewing God's covenant love—can hold meaning in an interpretation of this eschatological ecstasy. God's presence among the people will make all the difference at every level.

Such divine presence will bring universal liberation from oppression, illness, and social ostracism, Zephaniah proclaims (vv. 18–19). Indeed, the vision of a utopian society is invoked to motivate the audience to change the status quo. And as if such a vision was not enough, a homecoming with fame and fortune awaits at the finale (v. 20).

The reading for this Third Sunday in Advent harvests the climax of the book of Zephaniah, while the book as a whole feasts on juxtapositions. There is Jerusalem the unfaithful and corrupt placed alongside Jerusalem the city of universal rejoicing and justice; there is the contrast between idolatrous and purified—a city of violence versus a dove (that is, a city of peace). Within the book of Zephaniah, without the context of judgment and impending destruction, the concluding promises do not make sense.

What does that mean for Advent? What happens when this passage, frequently preached during Advent, is heard without its context? Or put theologically, what meaning does promise have without preceding judgment? Frankly, it remains shallow, like Pollyanna. Notably, throughout the Bible, promise does not come separated from judgment and suffering. Biblical writers have not offered comfort to the comfortable. Rather, eschatological passages succeed instances of death, destruction, and despair. Those who are oppressed now will be rejoicing in justice.

Thus, while certainly all congregations need occasions for celebration, the crucial connection between judgment and promise in this Advent text needs to be made clear. To do otherwise would be to deprive their hearers of the depth of the biblical message.

ANGELA BAUER-LEVESQUE

HOMILETICAL PERSPECTIVE

A first reading of this passage inspires thoughts of a word of hope in the mist of despair, a word of God's sure and strong promise to lift up those who are bowed down. It would be easy (and perhaps beneficial) to preach an end to fear and the rejoicing of those who are saved and protected by the Lord.

But how do we hear this word authentically in our context? How do we hear words of promise spoken to a people in exile in our own situation? Words of promise and restoration were spoken through Zephaniah to people who knew national devastation, who knew isolation from community and home. Privileged people in twenty-first-century North America hear these same words from a perspective of ease and comfort. We may and do experience the fears that war arouses, personal fears and anxieties, but it cannot be denied that our own experience is very different from that of Zephaniah's original hearers. It would be too easy to apply Zephaniah's words directly to our dis-eases and our dis-comforts.

So where can we enter this text? Where can we see ourselves in it? How can we hear this promise as authentic good news? Perhaps the first step is to recognize and to help people to understand a bit about the challenge in hearing this text. Perhaps we need to talk just a bit about our situation and about the situation of Israel in Zephaniah's time, so that we are all on the same page about the historical and cultural distance we face as we hear this text and attempt to understand what it might mean for us.

It might be helpful to begin a treatment of this text with a brief (re)telling of some of the historical and cultural context of the prophet. Whether written before or after the conquest of Judah by Babylon, this text was written in the context of that event or its threat. This text was first heard as a part of a divine judgment against Jerusalem. Earlier portions of Zephaniah speak out forcefully against the people of Jerusalem, promising retribution for their lack of faith. In this text itself, Zephaniah looks beyond the punishment to the restoration. This cycle of punishment and restoration is key to God's relationship with God's people, from the beginning of Genesis down to the present day. God will always restore. There is good news for any day and for any age.

The people to whom Zephaniah spoke this word were experiencing profound challenges. Their nation was embarrassed on the international scene: they were a pawn in the movements of the great world powers Babylon, Assyria, and others. Foreign armies were a constant threat and sometime reality. Lack of food and water, the basic necessities of life, accompanied this instability.

It is into this reality that Zephaniah speaks of restoration and an end to shame. Zephaniah promises not only an end to shame: Zephaniah promises that Israel will be praised throughout all the earth. What a radical promise this was to the fearful lot who first heard it!

After recognizing the profound differences between our own situation and that of Zephaniah's Israel, two interrelated approaches lend themselves to a hearing of this text as authentic good news for our time. We could first approach it from the context of our own challenges and fears and shames. If God can restore the fortunes to a nation bowed down before the powers of the world and dragged away into slavery, then God can also banish our fears and our challenges.

In a related way, we also may want to proclaim the universality of this promise. God's promised messianic kingdom and restoration of fortunes are not just for us and for our challenges. They are for the whole world. In God's messianic kingdom, oppressors will be dealt with (v. 19), because there will be no oppressed and no oppressors. In God's messianic kingdom, all the lame and the outcast will be restored. There will no "in groups" and "out groups," there will be no favored nations and unfavored nations. There will be no scattered nations and refugees, for all of God's people will be brought home and gathered (v. 20).

This kind of proclamation takes seriously the privileged position from which we North Americans hear this text. We largely do not experience extreme deprivation or shame, but because we love the world, we listen to that pain in the peoples of other nations and other classes. Then, informed and compassionate, we can pray in solidarity with our sisters and brothers around the world who do experience the world in ways much more like the experience of Zephaniah's hearers. We pray for an end to all disasters and conflicts, and we trust in God's promise for restoration.

As we pray in solidarity with our sisters and brothers around the world, we recognize that God's promise is also for us. At the end of the day, once we have recognized the differences between our own fears and the fears originally addressed by Zephaniah, we can say that God will banish our fears as well. God will ultimately bring an end to our pain and our suffering, whatever nature that pain and suffering take.

It is not inauthentic to claim the promise of restoration for ourselves as well. God brings good news to all people through the promise of Messiah and the final kingship of the Lord (v. 15). The good news is for the privileged of this world, as well as for those bowed down in this world. The good news is a promise of restoration to right relationships. When God promises that we will be praised throughout the world, the promise is based on who we are as God's children, and not on our own might or strength. When we are in right relationship with one another and with God, then we will be renowned and praised in all the earth (v. 20).

SETH MOLAND-KOVASH

Mark 13:24–37

THEOLOGICAL PERSPECTIVE

Does this text predict the future? If so, whose future? When? I shall argue, first, that Mark 13 anticipates multiple futures. Second, it reflects a common apocalyptic scenario about how God works. Third, the apocalyptic visions that present this scenario are recycled for new contexts; as such, they are comments on present circumstances more than predictions of future events. All this means that, fourth, we must understand how our context today may be similar to ancient contexts, so we may discern how to be faithful people of God in our time.

From the standpoint of the historical Jesus, "the Son of Man coming in clouds" (v. 26) sounds like the resurrection. Indeed, Christian theology sees the resurrection as a definitive, eschatological event. And this makes sense of 14:62, where Jesus offers the same saying to the high priest, who is looking for an excuse to have him put to death.

From the standpoint of Mark's original readers around 70 CE, much of this speech sounds like commentary on the Jewish revolt against Rome and the destruction of Jerusalem. After Jesus' prediction that the temple would be destroyed (13:2), the speech responds to the question, "When?" (13:4). The Jewish revolt is the most plausible historical context for Jesus' warning to flee (13:14) and his woes to women who are pregnant or nursing "in those days" (13:17). And the calamitous events of 70 CE account for Jesus' statement that "this generation will not pass away until all these things have taken place" (30).

From our standpoint today, however, 70 CE hardly qualifies as the end, no matter how traumatic that year was at the time. We might notice, therefore, that Jesus predicts not one but multiple wars and calamities (13:7–8). Also, the Son of Man "will gather his elect . . . from the ends of the earth" (13:27). This sounds like preparation for the judgment. Further, verse 32 ("about that day or hour no one knows") seems to rule out a date in 70 CE. And again, Jesus urges, "What I say to you I say to all" (13:37), indicating that his words apply beyond his immediate circle of disciples to Mark's readers, even to us.

So the predictions in this speech seem ambiguous, applicable to multiple circumstances. How, then, do we make sense of them? We must notice that the "Son of Man coming in clouds" (13:26) is from Daniel 7:13, and the "desolating sacrilege" (13:14) is from Daniel 9:27; 11:31; 12:11 (cf. 1 Macc. 1:54; 2 Macc. 6:1–6). Mark instructs us to pay attention to Daniel ("let the reader understand," v. 14). What we have in Mark 13 is a basic apocalyptic scenario lifted from Daniel and applied to new situations. The basic message of apocalyptic visions is this: The rebellion against the reign of God is strong, as the wicked oppress the righteous. Things will get worse before they get better. But hang on just a little longer, because just when you are sure you cannot endure, God will intervene to turn the world right side up.

In Mark 13, things are bad, and they will get worse. The "end is still to come" (v. 7); this is "the beginning of the birth pangs" (v. 8); "suffering, such as has not been from the beginning of the creation" (v. 19). It will feel like the cosmos is falling apart (vv. 24–25). But before things become unbearable God will "cut short those days" (v. 20).

In 167 BCE, the Seleucid emperor Antiochus IV Epiphanes banned all foreign religions. For Jews, that meant no circumcision and no sacrifices. It was illegal even to own a copy of Torah. In the context of the Maccabean revolt against Antiochus, the author of Daniel reached back into Jewish lore and recovered stories of the slave Daniel, who kept his faith in a pagan land even under threat of death. The book of Daniel exploits an analogy between the Babylonian oppression of Jews in the sixth century BCE and the Seleucid oppression of Jews in the second century BCE. So also Mark exploits analogies between the Seleucid oppression and the Roman oppression of God's people in the first century.

Apocalyptic visions are always available to be recycled and applied to new situations. The point is not to predict specific events in the future. Rather, apocalyptic theologians look to understand God's mighty acts in the past as a framework for understanding how the people of God should respond to the present. It turns out that the enemy is not any one empire; but all political and economic powers are liable to be co-opted by Satan.[6] They seek their own, worldly agendas at the expense of ordinary people.

The theologian must find analogies between the present and past circumstances in which God acted decisively, as recorded in Scripture. From

---

6. "Satan" is a metaphor for the negative (fallen) form of what Walter Wink calls "the inner aspect of material or tangible manifestations of power" (*Naming the Powers* [Philadelphia: Fortress Press, 1984], 104). For thoughtful analysis of how to confront fallen powers, see Wink, *Engaging the Powers* (Minneapolis: Fortress Press, 1992).

an apocalyptic perspective, we might ask, How does Satan try to influence every situation? How does God remain faithful in the midst of a crisis that is spiraling out of control? How can people of God tell the difference between following Satan and following God in any situation?

Amid the smoke of battle, the fog of politics, the confusion of economic distress, the babble of would-be leaders wearing God masks and claiming divine authority, how shall we know which way to turn? God's people should not be surprised or confused, because Jesus warned us ahead of time that such things would happen.

The powers that be will lull us to sleep by reassuring us that they have our best interests at heart as they pursue their worldly agendas. They play to our fears, our prejudices, our self-interests, so we do not notice their demonic behaviors. Beware. Keep alert. Keep awake (vv. 33, 35). The one who endures to the end will be saved (v. 13).

CHRISTOPHER R. HUTSON

PASTORAL PERSPECTIVE

Most congregations do not need to be told to "keep awake" during Advent. They are already operating in a state of sleep deprivation. At a church in the western suburbs of Chicago, nobody could accuse us of being asleep at the wheel. Rather, we might be accused of scurrying and overscheduling, running but getting nowhere, like bourgeois bunnies on the rabbit wheel. As Advent begins, the fall season has swept us through the "back to school season" of taking children to sports practices, choir rehearsals, and dance lessons. The church has aped the rhythm of the world, with programs now in full gear, from youth groups to adult studies and festive events. And now, suddenly, the rush of Advent.

With all there is to get ready for the holidays, secularly and sacredly, nobody needs to tell us to "keep awake." As a pastor, it strikes me this may instead be the season to pass out the sleeping pills or the chamomile tea, to a revved-up, overcaffeinated culture of busy-ness.

But let us be clear that while the world's busy-ness may seem to be pointed toward Christmas, it is seldom pointed toward the coming Christ child. As Advent progresses, the number of shopping days left before the big day offers a countdown that stresses us out and keeps us up late. These days we are startled into extra hours of wakefulness in a liturgical season that annoyingly presumes we might be asleep. No wonder we tune it out, like teenagers hearing a parent's repetitive lecture and knowing that mom simply does not understand.

But of course, God does understand. In this way, the Scripture from long ago reads us, not the other way around. In Advent, we are indeed asleep to much of what matters.

Like people who have lived by the train tracks for years, we no longer hear the sound of the train. After years in church, we get used to the noise of Advent, to the coming of Christ, so much so that we no longer notice it. Or if we do, it has ceased to jolt us awake and has become instead a low, dull rumble.

As children, when we first learned of Advent, we anxiously awaited the Christmas pageant, and even the God it pointed to. But now tired parents might see that pageant as one more activity to drive the kids to, in a busy week. New members who have been away from sacramental life return to the season of Advent with delight and wonder as the purple banners and Advent wreath appear. But after a few years, these signs of the season become mere decoration.

Like the house hunter who noticed the train tracks on moving day, but later sleeps through the whistles and the engines that rush by, we can miss the thing in the season of Advent that might have been most obvious and important at one time—the coming of Christ.

We may not be physically asleep; quite the opposite. But in our wakefulness to worldly ways, we fall asleep to the spiritual season, and so we need a wake-up call from the Gospel of Mark.

It is a strange wake-up call for people who no longer hold fig trees as key metaphors in our cultural life. When we do encounter figs, they tend to be mashed inside that moist little comfort food cookie, or we might have a fig alongside a piece of fine cheese.

But as for the fig trees themselves, I do not see any on the carefully mowed lawns outside Chicago. If we do mow our lawns, rake our leaves, it is as a chore, often for appearance's sake. We do not normally find ourselves considering the branches of the fig tree and how they produce or do not produce fruit. Fruit production happens at the grocery store, when we take the food from shelf, to bag, to car trunk, to pantry; and then suddenly, on our granite countertops, fruit has been "produced."

Yet most of us long for a richer sense of how fruit comes into the world, with its rhythms of leaves and seasons. So whether we walk in orchards or drive around the suburbs, the image of the fig tree transports us to another world. There we imagine people who tend branches, not for the fun of it or to decorate a garden that decorates a house. We imagine a place where fruit trees are tended to because they make a difference in our survival. We imagine a time when figs were a regular part of the diet and helped fill stomachs that might have been left empty, if someone had not faithfully tended those branches.

In a season that is gearing us up to shop, we consider what it would mean to stay away and engage the natural world, rather than the world of neon malls and sales. This life is precious and unpredictable. Its seasons are short. Let us not have it slip away, only to realize that we spent it shopping.

On the Third Sunday of Advent, there is still time to wake up from that bad dream. There is still time to encounter instead the presence of Christ in our waking hours.

An agricultural, natural image pulls no punches. The seasons pass, and the fig tree's growth follows an order, but that fig tree is fragile itself. Some figs will not make it; they simply will not flourish. Staying awake matters, not so much to protect ourselves, but also to notice the beauty in the moment. By staying awake, we may catch the second when the branch is tender, and learn that summer is near. By staying awake, we may be there to see the master who arrives when we are least expecting it, at midnight, at cockcrow, or at dawn.

Amidst the holiday parties and late-night shopping trips, the gospel reminds us to be awake to God in the world. This is a way of being awake that might actually be restful, and give us peace.

LILLIAN DANIEL

EXEGETICAL PERSPECTIVE

Watching and Waiting. "It is the end of the world as we know it" is not simply the stuff of twentieth-century rock song lyrics or twenty-first-century televangelist sermons. Ideas inherent in both apocalypticism and eschatology can be found in today's gospel lesson.[7] The phenomenon of apocalypticism grows out of difficult political and social crises; thus, it is no surprise that an apocalyptic mind-set is reflected in the writings of the postexilic era of Israel. As the Judeans grapple first with Babylonian, then Persian, Greek, and Roman oppressors, the covenant theology of the prophetic era gives way to an apocalyptic worldview, as writings such as 4 Ezra, *2 Baruch*, and Daniel attest.

Scholars debate the origins of the worldview or mind-set known as apocalypticism; they also debate the constitutive elements of the literary genre known as an apocalypse; however, it is generally agreed that both include elements of dualism (good versus evil); pessimism (times are extremely

7. Eschatology as a technical term was not coined until the nineteenth century, but apocalyptic thinking is often filled with talk of the end times.

tough); and imminence (so tough, in fact, that the world as we know it is about to end).[8] This final tenet, imminence, is related to the concept of eschatology, the doctrine of the end times. Apocalyptic reflections often address the imminence of judgment and the hope of better times ahead.

Today's Gospel lesson is from a chapter often referred to as "the little apocalypse." The material in Mark 13 is a narrative break in the Gospel, set between Mark's recounting of Jesus' teaching on the temple mount (Mark 12) and the passion narrative (Mark 14–16). In the opening verses of chapter 13, Jesus predicts the destruction of the temple and then, crossing over to the Mount of Olives, he begins to talk with Peter, James, John, and Andrew about the end of the age. Mark 13:5b–23 comprises a series of warnings regarding false indicators of the end. Jesus admonishes his disciples to watch and wait, for the end will come and they must be alert. The Gospel reading for this third Sunday in Advent is the second half of this chapter, and easily divides into three sections: Mark 13:24–27; Mark 13:28–31; and Mark 13:32–36.

Cosmic Signs. In the first section, the author shifts the readers' attention from false prophets and deceptive omens to the actual signs of the times. With apocalyptic imagery borrowed from Isaiah (13:10; 34:4); Joel (2:10; 3:4; 4:15); Ezekiel (32:7, 8); and Daniel (7:13), the evangelist employs a common trope of disturbances in the cosmic order to herald a significant event. It is not unusual in apocalyptic writing to call on cosmic imagery to describe the indescribable; in this instance it is the coming of the Son of Man that is spotlighted. Just as Isaiah, Joel, and Ezekiel use cosmic imagery to predict divine judgment, and just as Daniel writes of the coming Son of Man, here the evangelist creates a synthesis of images and allusions from the biblical tradition for the readers/hearers of the first century.

Lesson from the Fig Tree. An earlier story of the fig tree (Mark 11:20–22) focused on the destruction of the temple; Mark 13:28–31 is a short parable about a fig tree with the focus not on an end but on a beginning, offering hope in the imminence of the coming of the Son of Man. Just as the fig tree is the harbinger of summer, so will the signs Jesus is describing portend the coming of the Son of Man. One difficulty in this section lies in the statement in Mark 13:30, "this generation will not pass away until all these things have

8. For an excellent analysis of apocalypticism in antiquity, see David Hellholm, ed., *Apocalypticism in the Mediterranean World and the Near East: Proceedings of the International Colloquium on Apocalypticism, Uppsala, August 12–17, 1979* (Tübingen: J. C. B. Mohr [Paul Siebeck], 1983).

taken place" (reminiscent of Jesus' words in Mark 9:1). Although some of the events were realized by the first century, not all were. It is not unlikely that the qualifications offered in verse 31 come from the Markan era as the community grappled with the delay of the coming.

Parabolic Warning. The closing parable of chapter 13, the story of a man on a journey, seems to serve several purposes in the narrative. Just as Mark 13:31 seems to reflect the evangelist's attempt to deal with the delay of the Parousia, so too does Mark 13:32 call the hearer to think beyond the moment because "about that day or hour no one knows." The lessons here admonish the hearer to be more concerned with being prepared and alert than with knowing the day or hour.

In addition to offering a window onto the audience of Mark's Gospel and their concern over the delay of the second coming, the parable in this final section of chapter 13 also serves a proleptic function in the narrative. Note, for example, how in verse 35 Jesus warns his listeners to "keep awake," because the time of the return of the master is unknown; it could be "in the evening, or at midnight, or at cockcrow, or at dawn." Here in the close of this narrative break is a foreshadowing of significant elements in the passion narrative to follow.

A Word for Today. This Gospel reading fits well with many other readings for Advent in that it carries the theme of waiting. In this Advent season we must watch and wait! As we move through the season, as we move closer to the coming of the Christ child, the admonition to be alert once again cries out across time and space. With the people of the texts we cry out this Advent season, "Where are you, God? When are you coming? Come now." Jesus reminds us now, as he reminded them then, that he will come again. We need not get lost in the details. Better to concentrate on being ready.

JUDY YATES SIKER

HOMILETICAL PERSPECTIVE

This passage, which is a portion of what is often called "the little apocalypse," puts us in the presence of the adult Jesus offering both prophetic judgment and prophetic comfort. He anticipates the end times when heaven will literally quake and stars will begin to fall out of the sky. What sounds like a disaster, however, actually prepares the way for the "Son of Man" and his gathering of the elect. This text follows the advice of epic movie director Cecil B. De Mille: "Start with an earthquake, then build to a climax." Certainly, from the very first word, there can be no doubt that there is much at stake in this season, and in the very beginning of this story we are given a glimpse of its ending.

It can seem strange, at first, to be exhorted to wait for his coming again when, in the context of the liturgical year, we are still awaiting his birth. In one important respect, however, it is entirely fitting, because it places us squarely with those who awaited the birth of the Messiah. Neither those who awaited the first coming of the Messiah, nor those who now await his return, know when he will appear.

In other respects, our contemporary anticipation of the coming of God's Promised One at Christmas is quite different from the experience of those who awaited the Messiah. After all, we know whom we are waiting for. We know the day he will arrive. It is circled in red on our calendars. We have Advent calendars and Advent candles to help us count down to the promised day.

By contrast, of course, those who lived before the birth of Jesus did not know the day or the hour of his arrival, so they needed to live in a continual state of watchfulness. The birth of the Messiah could only be celebrated as a surprise party that could take place on any day, at any moment. By anticipating the return of the Son of Man here, at the beginning of Advent, we wait in the same way those who lived before Jesus was born waited, not knowing the day or the hour when the Messiah would appear. We also join them in hearing—and needing—the same exhortation to be watchful and to keep awake.

A preacher might approach this text by considering the differences between waiting for Christmas and waiting for Christ. Obviously, we know when Christmas will arrive and what it will be like when it does. We know the script, and all we need do is follow it. But waiting for Christ to come—or to come again—requires something more, an expectant watchfulness, because we never know when he will appear.

This requires from us a different kind of waiting. Some waiting is passive. But there is also active waiting. A girl who stands on a street corner waiting for the bus to arrive will experience one kind of waiting, a passive waiting. That same girl on the same corner hearing the sound of a parade that is just out of sight will also wait, but it will be a different kind of waiting, full of expectation, a waiting on tiptoe, an active waiting.

A fisherman finds it burdensome to wait for spring to arrive because it is a passive waiting. Once he is fishing, however, he does not find it a burden to wait for the trout to rise to his fly because it is an active kind of waiting, full of expectation. At the pool of his favorite trout stream his waiting is filled with accomplishing all the many things he must do, all injected with an active sense of anticipation because he never knows when the trout may appear. That is the kind of active waiting Jesus had in mind when he enjoined his followers, "Beware, keep alert; for you do not know when the time will come" (Mark 13:33).

It is clear that Jesus does not intend for us to predict when he will return. Rather, he is urging us to live as if his return were just around the corner. So there is no time to nod off in a waiting room. Rather, we are to be more like a waiter who is continually busy in serving others and so has no time to sit down and count the tips.

At the same time, we are to be attuned to the signs of his rule around us, because, indeed, he has already arrived. It would be a mistake to preach so persuasively about awaiting Christ's return that listeners might forget, for a moment at least, that he came in the first place.

This text forces the preacher to wade into one of the most important paradoxes of the gospel: the "already/not yet" quality to the portion of the divine drama in which we live. *Already* Jesus has established the means through which we are drawn into relationship with God, but *not yet* do we live in complete communion with God. *Already* the realm of God is evident, but *not yet* is that realm fully established.

In this portion of Mark's Gospel Jesus addresses those who have to live in the meantime, the challenging meantime between the "already" and the "not yet." By keeping alert and awake, by living our lives in accord with the One who has already come, died, and been raised, not only will we be prepared to live in the promised realm of God when it comes, but we may experience even now some of what life in the realm will be like.

MARTIN B. COPENHAVER

Fourth Sunday of Advent

Psalm 146:5–10

⁵Happy are those whose help is the God of Jacob,
   whose hope is in the Lord their God,
⁶who made heaven and earth,
   the sea, and all that is in them;
who keeps faith forever;
   ⁷who executes justice for the oppressed;
   who gives food to the hungry.

The Lord sets the prisoners free;
   ⁸the Lord opens the eyes of the blind.
The Lord lifts up those who are bowed down;
   the Lord loves the righteous.
⁹The Lord watches over the strangers;
   he upholds the orphan and the widow,
   but the way of the wicked he brings to ruin.

¹⁰The Lord will reign forever,
   your God, O Zion, for all generations.
Praise the Lord!

Luke 1:46b–55

"My soul magnifies the Lord,
   ⁴⁷and my spirit rejoices in God my Savior,
⁴⁸for he has looked with favor on the lowliness of his servant.
   Surely, from now on all generations will call me blessed;
⁴⁹for the Mighty One has done great things for me,
   and holy is his name.
⁵⁰His mercy is for those who fear him
   from generation to generation.
⁵¹He has shown strength with his arm;
   he has scattered the proud in the thoughts of their hearts.

^{52}He has brought down the powerful from their thrones,
and lifted up the lowly;
^{53}he has filled the hungry with good things,
and sent the rich away empty.
^{54}He has helped his servant Israel,
in remembrance of his mercy,
^{55}according to the promise he made to our ancestors,
to Abraham and to his descendants forever."

ORDER OF WORSHIP

OPENING WORDS / CALL TO WORSHIP

My soul magnifies the Lord;   *Luke 1:46b–47*
my spirit rejoices in God my Savior.
The Mighty One has done great things.   *Luke 1:49*
Holy is God's name!

LIGHTING OF THE ADVENT CANDLES

[Reader 1]: We light this candle as a symbol of the
joy to be found in your kingdom on earth.
[Reader 2]: For the Lord elevates the lowly, releases
the captive, and brings sight to the blind.
We rejoice in his justice and mercy, faithful
to all generations.
[All]: **Come, Lord Jesus, come!**

HYMN, SPIRITUAL, OR PSALM

CALL TO CONFESSION

Happy are those whose help is the Lord.   *Ps. 146:1*
Let us seek God's help as we confess our sins.

PRAYER OF CONFESSION

God our Savior, we ask for your mercy.   *Luke 1:46b–55*
Though we have heard Mary's song,
we still seek security in pride and power and
possessions.
Though we know your story,
we resist the costs of following you.

We pass by those considered lowly in this world.
We turn away from hungry people who still wait
    to be filled.
Forgive us, we pray.
Help us to work for the justice you intend.
Make us messengers of the peace you bring.
As we wait for you, turn our apathy into acts of love and service.
We pray in the name of Jesus Christ, Emmanuel. Amen.

DECLARATION OF FORGIVENESS

God forgives all our sins
and promises to bring us to everlasting life.
Thanks be to God!

PRAYER OF THE DAY

God, our light and our salvation,
you bring hope and peace
to the lowly and oppressed.
Let us see the world through your eyes
that we may love the widow and orphan,   *Ps. 146:7, 9*
that we may work for justice,
that our lives may bear witness to the good news
of the kingdom at hand
and our vocation serve to draw people to your salvation;
through your Son, Jesus Christ, in the power
of the Holy Spirit. **Amen.**

HYMN, SPIRITUAL, OR PSALM

PRAYER FOR ILLUMINATION

O Mighty One,   *Luke 1:51, 53*
who scatters the proud
and fills the hungry,
by your Holy Spirit
let your word leap in us
and bring to our yearning
the joy that comes with
new beginnings and renewed lives. **Amen.**

SCRIPTURE READINGS

SERMON

HYMN, SPIRITUAL, OR PSALM

PRAYERS OF INTERCESSION

Remember your mercy, O Lord, and help us,   *Luke 1:46–55*
according to the promise of your steadfast love.

Let all generations see your blessing,
for your name is holy and your mercy is great.

Show the strength of your hand,
and lift the burdens of the poor.

Work wonders for the humble,
and scatter the plans of the proud.

Look with favor on the lowly,
and cast down tyrants from their thrones.

Fill the hungry with good things,
and empty the hands of the greedy.

Then we will sing out with joy and glorify you forever;
through Jesus Christ our Savior. Amen.

LORD'S PRAYER

INVITATION TO THE OFFERING

God, the source of all good things,
has given us what we need.
In joyful response, let us offer our gifts,
the fruit of our labors, and the dedication of our hearts
for loving service in the name of Christ.

PRAYER OF THANKSGIVING/DEDICATION

Thanks be to you, O God, maker of heaven and earth—   *Ps. 146:5–10*
giver of justice, lover of righteousness,

hope of the afflicted, and friend of the poor.
Your faithfulness never fails.
Take and use these gifts we offer
to further your purpose in the world
and to fulfill the promise of the world to come;
through Christ our Lord we pray. **Amen.**

HYMN, SPIRITUAL, OR PSALM

CHARGE

Remember what the Lord has done for you   *Luke 1:49*
and for all the peoples of the earth.

BLESSING

Bless the Lord with all your soul,   *Luke 1:46b, 48*
and may the blessing of God be with you.

SONG SUGGESTIONS

"For You, O Lord, My Soul in Stillness Waits" (*GC* 328, *GTG* 89)
"Light One Candle to Watch for Messiah," stanza 4 (*ELW* 240, *GTG* 85)
"My Soul Cries Out with a Joyful Shout" (*ELW* 723, *GC* 556, *GTG* 100)
"My Soul Gives Glory to My God" (*CH* 130–131, *GTG* 99, *TNCH* 119, *UMH* 198)
"O Lord, How Shall I Meet You" (*ELW* 241, *GTG* 104, *TNCH* 102)
"The Angel Gabriel from Heaven Came" (*ELW* 265)
"The People Who Walked in Darkness" (*GTG* 86)
"To a Maid Whose Name Was Mary" (*GTG* 98, *UMH* 215)

CHILDREN'S SERMON

Based on Luke 1:39–55

First, there was Zechariah and Elizabeth, a couple who lived out in the Judean hill country. They were too old to have children, or so they thought. The angel Gabriel told Zechariah when he was on duty in the temple that his wife, Elizabeth, would have a baby boy. They were to name the baby John. Now they were waiting for the baby to be born.

Second, there was Mary, a teenage girl who lived in Nazareth. She was engaged to Joseph. But out of nowhere the angel Gabriel told her that she was going to have a baby boy too! She was to name the baby Jesus. Now she and Joseph were waiting for the baby to be born.

Elizabeth and Mary were related, but we are not sure how. Before Gabriel left Mary, he told her that Elizabeth was going to have a baby boy too. So Mary decided to go visit Elizabeth. Now this was not a walk next door for a cup of tea. No, this was a very long walk, and Mary planned to stay with Elizabeth and Zechariah for a while.

When Mary got to their house, she called out to Elizabeth. "Elizabeth! It's Mary! I have come to see you!" How surprised Elizabeth must have been! In those days, you could not call or e-mail or text someone to say, "I'm coming to see you next week," so it was a big surprise.

When Elizabeth heard Mary's voice, the baby boy inside Elizabeth jumped. And at that moment, Elizabeth was filled with God's Holy Spirit.

"God has blessed you above all women," Elizabeth shouted. "Your baby is blessed too. How honored I am that you have come to see me. My baby leaped with joy when I heard your voice."

Mary praised God with all her heart, saying,

"God is great and mighty!
God is loving and strong!
We belong to God.
We can count on God to help us."

Mary stayed with Elizabeth for many days, and then she went back home to Nazareth to wait for the time when her baby would be born.

Prayer: Thank you for faithful mothers who honor God and love their babies. Amen.

SERMON HELPS

Psalm 146:5–10

THEOLOGICAL PERSPECTIVE

Psalm 146 is one of the so-called Hallelujah psalms that wrap up the Psalms. The text begins with "Hallelujah!" This one word sums up all human response of praise to the God who has created, as Martin Luther put it, "me and all things." Its music gives birth to many songs. For many, "Hallelujah" will bring to mind the chorus from George Frideric Handel's *Messiah*.

However, the version that resonates with contemporary people both inside and outside the church is Leonard Cohen's song "Hallelujah."

Cohen's version has been covered by more than 100 other artists, including Jeff Buckley, Rufus Wainwright, k. d. lang, U2, and Bob Dylan, to name just a few. Why does Cohen's poem-psalm resonate so broadly in popular culture today? In part, the song allows for complexity, acknowledging both the glorious heights of the "holy hallelujah" and our failings that make necessary a "broken hallelujah." Finally, despite all the brokenness of our lives, Cohen claims the bold stance of standing before the Lord of song and singing his praise to the Lord of song. It is as if the promise rings out in the midst of brokenness. God's will for good, for a life of shalom, of both well-doing and doing well, evokes praise, and in the praise arises hope.

What sense does it make to speak of a broken hallelujah when the text clearly says, "happy are those whose help is in the LORD" (v. 5)? Happy, as Bob Dylan once remarked, is a yuppie word. In the first instance, this text, despite the translation of its first word, is not about happiness. At least it is not about happiness in the sense shared by most people in the developed nations of the West, oriented as they are to individuals rationally pursuing life, liberty, and the pursuit of happiness. No, happiness here is about flourishing. From ancient times, the stark choice has been set before the people of God: walk the way of life or the way of death. This psalm is about walking the way of life. Deep gladness may get at the sensibility of life lived in response to the God described in this psalm.

So when one hears about hope in the Lord as this reading unfolds, by association it is easy to hear the opposite, the broken hope that comes when we put trust in leaders. This psalm, and many like it, rises from the tension between the broken and the holy hallelujah. The biblical witness is not that leaders should be automatically opposed; in fact, they are desperately needed. The issue is rather in trusting rightly, and passage after passage witnesses to the trustworthiness of God rather than human leaders. In fact, one could say that the season of Advent as a whole arises from the tension between the broken realities of actual leadership and the holy trustworthiness of God.

This section of the psalm (and similar texts such as Isa. 35 and Matt. 11) offers what one might call a resume of what we can expect when we trust in God. Put better, these few verses offer us a testimony to the basis of God's trustworthiness. That basis begins in a claim of power. This is emphatically not the God of any one tribe or nation, not the pet deity of any prosperity seeker or power grabber. This god is God of all creation, maker of sky, earth, water, and all that lives in them. There is, to paraphrase the Reformed theologian and former prime minister of the Netherlands Abraham Kuyper, not one square inch of all creation over which the Lord does not say, "Mine!"

The creator of all has power beyond measure, yet its exercise does not take the form or character of a tyrant, someone whom we must bribe for our petitions and prayers to be answered. Rather, this powerful God has already taken sides in history, responding to the cries of those in great need, responding with great mercy and transforming love.

The litany is familiar and deeply comforting to all who feel pressed down by the broken power and untrustworthy leadership of this world. The oppressed will finally receive justice; the hungry will be fed; those held in bondage will be freed; the blind will find new sight; those broken down by the weight of their worries will find their load lifted; and the righteous, often despised by the world, will find the Lord of all creation present to them in overwhelming love. If this were not clear enough evidence in the courtroom, offering a witness to the character of this God of power and majesty, we find that this God tends those most marginal, most vulnerable: the stranger, the orphan, the widow. Today, it might be a lonely AIDS orphan in Ethiopia or an undocumented immigrant sweating in a hot restaurant kitchen in New York or a scorching field in California.

While God loves the poor, caring for them in particularly tender and specific ways, God also has a strong word for the wicked. Wicked lives are brought to ruin in many ways, but the most significant may be the tears of recognition at the end of life, when one faces the inhumanity of one's own privilege. It is a wretched ruin when one sees, as does Dickens's Scrooge, how stone-hearted hoarding creates its own hell.

More people fall into this hell today than we care to admit. Thus it can be argued that this psalm comes as a critique of leaders, of those in power, of those with wealth and success, asking them how their use of power matches up to God's own character. Does their leadership bend toward mercy as does that of the Lord of space and time? As well, it asks all of us to assess our trust making—even with leaders who seem very noble. If our trust is placed in the Lord alone, we can continue to press our leaders to be trustworthy measured against the picture of God's desired shalom, our longed-for hope in the midst of this broken not-yet time.

CHRISTIAN SCHAREN

PASTORAL PERSPECTIVE

In Psalm 146 we are counselled to put our trust not in political leaders or mortal human beings, but rather in God. God is described as compassionate and just, trustworthy, and active in the world. The question before the preacher this Fourth Sunday of Advent is a faith-shaking one: Are these things *really true* in our experience, both preacher and parishioner? Can we trust God to act with justice and compassion in the real world and our real worlds?

This psalm draws a particular picture of God in the mind of the hearer. God is the creator of heaven, earth, and sea—and is therefore ultimately powerful in the world. God is faithful, just, and generous. God pays particular attention to those in need—giving food to the hungry, freedom to the prisoners, sight to the blind, safety and support to the vulnerable, a hand up for those who are bowed down. For judgment, the psalm says that God "loves the righteous" (v. 8) and brings "the *way of the wicked* . . . to ruin" (v. 9, my emphasis). On the one hand, this picture of God surprises no one. God is expected to wear the white hat, to be the embodiment of everything that we consider to be good. On the other hand, though, this picture stands in contrast to the way God is often viewed in the culture at large and, truth be told, in the depths of our own Christian hearts.

Richard Dawkins overstates the case, but likely speaks for many, when he writes:

> The God of the Old Testament is arguably the most unpleasant character in all fiction: jealous and proud of it; a petty, unjust, unforgiving control-freak; a vindictive, bloodthirsty ethnic cleanser; a misogynistic, homophobic, racist, infanticidal, genocidal, filicidal, pestilential, megalomaniacal, sadomasochistic, capriciously malevolent bully.[1]

In this Advent season, many in our pews do *not*, in their heart of hearts, believe that God is truly compassionate and just. A woman had just given birth to twins; one of them was stillborn and the other was in intensive care, balanced between life and death. Her first desperate question to her pastor was, "Was there something I did to deserve this?" Many fear God's judgment. Many carry guilt and assume that they are not good enough to be loved by God. Many, in the depths of their hearts, believe that they must be more righteous than they are in order to be loved by God, and that oppression, imprisonment, blindness, loneliness, and suffering are not occasions for God's care but the thin edge of God's condemnation.

Neither Dawkins nor the general populace pulls that harsh image of God out of thin air; suffering and injustice are very real, and the pictures of God

---

1. Richard Dawkins, *The God Delusion* (Boston: Mariner Books, 2008), 51.

presented in the Bible and by the church are, to say the least, complex. Contradictory images of God struggle in the depths of many, and perhaps most, of those who will hear Advent sermons this year. This psalm, so soon before we celebrate the out-of-wedlock stable birth (or the refugee flight) of the Messiah, presents an opportunity to present the good news of unconditional love, and a judgment that falls not upon the person of the wicked, but upon the *way of the wicked*.

That said, this psalm raises an even more troubling question. There are many in this world—and in our own pews—who find themselves in exactly the situations described here. The blind, the widowed, the hungry, the oppressed are called upon to trust God. Is God truly trustworthy? Does God act in tangible ways, bringing grace to the point of our need? Our people are asking that this Sunday.

It is all too easy for Richard Dawkins and his many sympathizers in and out of churches to say that God does *not* intervene in the lives of humanity. For examples, they bring up all those hungry who are *not* given food, all those vulnerable who are *not* protected, all those who are bowed down and *not* lifted up. The point is undeniable. Many in this world look to God for help, and the looked-for help never comes. Probably all of us know this experience at some level. Even Jesus knew this experience, on the cross. How can we honestly say that God is faithful and just, and *trustworthy?* If God is *not* pulling puppet strings or interfering with the laws of nature to rescue humanity in time of need, what *is* God doing? How does grace really operate in this real world?

Finally, there seems to be a challenge—and a promise—to our incarnational faith in this psalm, given the time of year. In what way does the church—the body of Christ—incarnate this grace and trustworthiness of God? Where once people could find healing by reaching out to touch the hem of Jesus' garment (Mark 5:25–34) can they now find healing by touching the community of the church?[2] Profoundly, is this true—not just for the masses who suffer out there, around the world, but for those who suffer right here in our midst in this place on this Sunday?

Psalm 146 is a powerful lead-in to the great surprise of Christmas, the birth of the Messiah in a stable, into poverty and oppression. It confronts us with the conflict and contradiction in our images of God. It forces us to look honestly and deeply for the grace of God, the true ways in which God is trustworthy, just, and compassionate. It asks us, as the gospel so often does,

2. For a very helpful discussion of this idea, see Ronald Rolheiser, *The Holy Longing* (New York: Doubleday, 1999).

to be the change we hope to see in the world. It prepares us for the surprise that God's grace will find us in the places where we are least deserving, and most in need.

DAVID HOLMES

EXEGETICAL PERSPECTIVE

In Hebrew, the book of Psalms is called *Tehillim*, or praises: an odd choice, given that there are far more prayers for help in the Psalter than songs of praise. However, the Psalms are divided into five parts by four doxologies, so that the book is punctuated with praise. Moreover, the book of Psalms concludes with a series of five rollicking songs of praise, beginning with the psalm for today, all incorporating the shout of praise *halleluyah* (rendered "Praise the LORD" in the NRSV; see 146:1, 10).[3] In this way, the last word of the book (quite literally; see Ps. 150:6!) becomes a word of praise, spoken in the face of trouble, need, and disaster.[4]

Although this psalm begins and ends with hallelujahs (vv. 1 and 10), it moves quickly to a contrast between earthly kings and the heavenly king. In contrast to other psalms (Psalm 72, for example), which in keeping with ancient Near Eastern traditions as well as biblical precedent regarded the king as guarantor of justice for the oppressed, Psalm 146 offers a warning:

> Do not put your trust in princes,
>   in mortals, in whom there is no help.
> When their breath departs, they return to the earth;
>   on that very day their plans perish.
>
> *(vv. 3–4)*

However exalted his station, the king remains mortal. Therefore, the institution of kingship is fundamentally flawed. Even assuming that his intentions are good, the king is subject to human weakness and failure; indeed, ultimately, every king *will* fail, because ultimately he will die, and his plans, for good or ill, will be left in the hands of others. To put it another way, kingship cannot bear the weight of ultimacy; no human institution can.

However, God does what the kings either could not, or would not, do. It is the Lord "who executes justice for the oppressed; who gives food to the

---

3. Gerald H. Wilson, "The Shape of the Book of Psalms," *Interpretation* 46 (1992): 132–33.
4. Jerome Creach writes that lament "gives evidence of faith worked out in the midst of hardship, hurt and loss. Perhaps this is the reason the editors of the Psalter labeled the book 'Praises,' even though it is dominated by the lament genre" ("Between Text and Sermon: Psalm 70," *Interpretation* 60 [2006]: 64).

hungry" (v. 7a). God's reign means freedom for the imprisoned, sight for the blind, exaltation for the humiliated (vv. 7b–8). It is God, not the king, who truly regards the plight of those without advocates—orphans, widows, refugees—and guarantees justice for them (vv. 8–9a). God is *willing* to act because "the LORD loves the righteous . . . but the way of the wicked he brings to ruin" (vv. 8b–9). God is *able* to act because he is the world's creator (v. 6). Unlike the mortal kings of David's line, God's rule is eternal. God can bear the weight of our trust and ultimate regard, for it is the Lord "who keeps faith forever" (v. 6b). Therefore, the psalmist acclaims God's rule:

The LORD will reign forever,
    your God, O Zion, for all generations.
(v. 10)

It is likely that Psalm 146 reflects the reconsideration of God's eternal covenant with David (see 2 Sam. 23:5; cf. also 2 Sam. 7:11b–16) in the time after the exile. Previously, it had been thought that the promise guaranteed the political survival of David's line forever (see, e.g., Ps. 89:35–37). Then Jerusalem fell to the Babylonians, and the succession ended with Zedekiah. Never again would a son of David sit on a throne in Jerusalem.

How was Israel to cope with this disaster? The Psalms respond theologically, by affirming God's reign over any and every false claim to authority over this world (see esp. the enthronement songs, Pss. 24, 29, 47, 93, 96, 97, 98, 99). Psalm 146 stands as a rebuke to the naiveté that had ascribed to the human institution of kingship an ultimacy that even the best and most noble king could not bear. Sadly, this temptation is still with us. Too often, Christians have identified the gospel unambiguously with some political party or movement, forgetting that faith's proper role is to critique all human authorities in light of the God made manifest in Jesus. Inevitably, such mistaken investitures of faith end in disillusionment and disappointment. Only God can, and ought to, bear the weight of our ultimate faith and commitment.

The Gospel reading suggested for today is Luke's Magnificat (Luke 1:46b–55). Like that well-known poem, Psalm 146 is an expression of God's passion for justice and special concern for the poor. Although it lacks the explicit reversals set forth in Mary's song, today's psalm involves an implicit reversal of status, through its contrast between untrustworthy princes and the trustworthy God. In Psalm 146, the righteous, however humble and oppressed, have God's care and regard, while the wicked, however powerful, earn God's enmity (v. 9).

The description of God's work for justice in Psalm 146:7–9 sounds much like the description of Jesus' ministry in the Gospel for today. Indeed, this parallel points us toward another solution to the problem posed by the end of Davidic kingship in Israel: the hope that one day, God would raise up a future descendant of David as Messiah, to usher in God's kingdom. The Christian confession that Jesus is Christ (the Greek *christos* is the equivalent of the Hebrew *mashiach*, or messiah) embraces this idea, though paradoxically: Jesus' identity is revealed through humble service, not through kingly pomp. So, when John the Baptist sends from prison for confirmation that Jesus truly is that promised one, the proof comes in Jesus' care for the needy: "the blind receive their sight, the lame walk, the lepers are cleansed, the deaf hear, the dead are raised, and the poor have good news brought to them" (Matt. 11:5).

God's reign means justice and deliverance, particularly for the least and forgotten. When we care for the needy, we act as the hands of Christ in our world and participate in God's coming kingdom here and now.

STEVEN S. TUELL

HOMILETICAL PERSPECTIVE

Today's psalm reveals how joy is found through reliance on God. The psalmist's words are flung aloft in high hopes for the help that God brings, and we see this demonstrated in swelling praises of God's *shalom*. The exalted words of happiness and the ensuing divine deeds are surely a testament that the psalmist's hope is well founded.

The key components of the psalm are hope, help, and happiness. They invite the preacher to reflect on the mutually influencing aspects of these powerful antidotes to a world in need of redemption.

Hope. There is no doubt that our world is a broken and hurting one—poverty ravages billions globally, preventing them from receiving proper nutrition, medical care, vaccinations, or shelter. Those oppressed by personal or societal injustice experience prejudice, discrimination, violence, or persecution, while others facing physical or psychological illness must struggle to find hope for personal comfort or restitution.

The psalmist reminds us that God recognizes the devastating effects of these realities and envisions a world reordered. Hence, we are told that justice is being rendered, prisoners released, the hungry fed, the sick healed, and society's most vulnerable sheltered (vv. 7–9). In the advent of Christ, that work has begun anew. So, looking to our world, we see the manifestations of it. In the abolitionist movement, slaves were freed because of the work of activists like Harriet Tubman, Harriet Beecher Stowe, and William Wilberforce; in the struggle against apartheid, racial equality began to be restored in South Africa because of leaders like Nelson Mandela and Desmond Tutu; and with the advent of medications such as the tuberculosis and polio vaccines, millions of lives have been saved.

Help. For us as Christians, empathy for the global problems that we face comes easily, but so does feeling overwhelmed. An empathic response is true to our nature, and yet we often feel helpless as individuals. What can we do that will make a difference?

It is perhaps most important for us to remember that this work must be accomplished not just at a personal level but at a communal one as well, and that our greatest strength is in numbers. After all, earth holds six billion people, and two billion consider themselves Christians—that is one-third of the global population. Together we can make a difference; the work of alleviating global poverty, oppression, and illness must be done not alone but in community.

One of the frustrating aspects of engaging in this work is that we often will not see the fruit of such labors in our lifetime. This makes it easy to believe that our work is for naught. Nevertheless it is our hope that our efforts will benefit those who come after us, a hope that rests in God, who "will reign forever . . . for all generations" (v. 10). In the meantime, there are many things that we can agree upon across belief systems to work toward the eradication of extreme poverty for the good of God's global family.

Tangible goals will help our hearers hope along with the psalmist. Many faith families have embraced the Millennium Development Goals (MDGs) as helpful tools to work toward God's vision of our world restored. These goals offer a series of poverty reduction targets that can help organize our action. Participating in programs that empower women and girls, support education, build healthy infrastructures, fund research for devastating diseases, and promote environmental sustainability can all help to build the reign the psalmist envisions.

To become part of God's work means being part of a biblical ethic in which God "loves the righteous" and the wicked are brought to ruin (vv. 8b, 9b). As J. Clinton McCann Jr. writes, "To be righteous is to trust that one's life fundamentally depends on God. . . . To be wicked means fundamentally to be self-ruled rather than God-ruled. In Biblical terms, wickedness means to be autonomous, which means literally to be a 'law unto oneself.'"[5]

5. J. Clinton McCann Jr., "Preaching on Psalms for Advent," *Journal for Preachers* 16, no. 4 (1992): 14–15.

Wickedness becomes essentially a question of allegiance: in whom or in what do we trust? In the advent of Christ, radical dependence is writ large in the poverty of the stable, just as it is in the agony of a garden. However, this kind of radical dependence on God and our community is counterintuitive in Western cultures that prize autonomy and independence.

Our mission, then, is one of interdependence in which we strive to participate with one another in God's mission. The work is not ours alone, nor can it be accomplished by us alone. In Africa this kind of interdependence is called *ubuntu*, which Desmond Tutu's words translate: "A person is a person *through* other persons."[6] As persons uniquely created in the image of God, we are truly ourselves only in relationship with others.

Happiness. Our happiness comes in recognizing our total dependence on God, and when we rely on God, joining in the global community working to alleviate poverty and other ills becomes easier. When we partner with our global family near or afar, we not only begin to combat our world's great problems; we also are enriched by the gifts of our neighbors, discover our interconnectedness, and come to know strangers as friends.

Finally, when we rely on God, joy is the result. Empowered by God, we can go into the world, engaging in right relationship with God and neighbor. We can therefore live in a reality that is both God-centered and other-centered. This rightful ordering of our relationships and our place in creation allows us to say yes to the life and labors before us. Therein lies our happiness.

CAROL L. WADE

Luke 1:46b–55

THEOLOGICAL PERSPECTIVE

The status quo does not obtain in God's economy. When God moves into the life of the world, everything changes. The old ordering of life is displaced in no uncertain terms, and a new ordering of life is put in its place. The old has gone, the new has come, and nothing will ever be the same again. Theologically, Advent means this: when God announces the divine intention to act decisively in the incarnation of the Word, everything gets turned on its head.

Mary's song of praise in response to her pregnancy and her awareness,

6. Desmond Tutu, *God Has a Dream: A Vision of Hope for Our Time* (New York: Random House, 2004), 25.

at least in part, of its theological significance are an expression of hope in the God of Israel now acting in eschatological power. The kingdom that has been promised in Israel's past is coming to pass. Advent announces its inauguration. The content of the new work of God is not given in lofty theological images but as the ethic of a changed world order. In concrete and specific terms, Mary sings in the language of revolution (a turning around) to record her understanding of the great reversals that have unfolded, albeit, we must add, in a hidden way. The effect of the "prophetic perfects," suggests Geoffrey Wainwright, may incite the reader, in political terms, to a "revolution of the left," as one aligns oneself with the revolutionary action of God.[7]

Before we look at the reversals, however, let us pause for a moment to reflect on the effect that God's acts have on Mary: her soul magnifies the Lord; her spirit rejoices in God her savior. Her inner knowledge of what God has done calls her to worship. The repetitive affirmation is a declaration of worship of the God in whom she delights. The act of Mary's worship reminds us that the hope for the reign of God is in the God who acts, who alone is worthy of praise. This immediately places the statements of the reversals in a context that is far more than the outline of a political manifesto. The reign of God no doubt has profound political implications, but political action, no matter how noble, does not inaugurate the reign of God. Nevertheless, there is content to the acts of God, and Mary's song is not bashful in announcing what may be summed up as good news for the poor and downtrodden, and as very bad news indeed for those who hitherto have wielded economic, political, and military power.

There are five reversals. The first is the reversal that Mary experiences herself. She is of low estate, a peasant girl, unmarried, living in an economically poor and militarily occupied country. Yet she is *theotokos*, God-bearer. Protestants can surely find a place in their piety for the celebration of Mary as a blessed woman, for the Mighty One did great things for her, and through her, for us. In no sense, of course, should we depict Mary as mediatrix, as having soteriological status. Yet as a woman who was singular in her vocation from God to carry the Son of God in utero, she is one for whom we thank God that God found such a one as her worthy. God's mercy is for those who fear God.

Second, God has acted with a strong arm to scatter the prideful. Pride has conventionally been seen as the core sin, from which arise all other aspects and expressions of a broken relationship with God and, consequently, with

---

7. Geoffrey Wainwright, *Doxology: The Praise of God in Worship, Doctrine, and Life* (New York: Oxford University Press, 1980), 426–27.

one another. Self-satisfied and gratuitous self-referencing is not what God wants from us. God's response to our pride has a military overtone, for God has scattered the proud by the wielding of a strong arm. With the same arm, God, third, has brought down the powerful from their thrones and lifted up those who are without status and rights. The images are violent and thrustful. Similarly, fourth, God has filled the hungry and sent the rich away with nothing. The reversals are dramatic, purposeful, and final. There is no ambiguity concerning what God has done.

The final reversal is more hidden. Israel, the servant of God, has throughout her history been the subject of God's judgment. Now, Israel is the recipient of God's mercy, as God remains faithful to promises made long ago. The people who angered God—they offended God's holiness and compassion; they violated God's love and justice—to them God shows mercy. God has helped Israel.

The issue now is to establish what the reversals mean. Certainly they are moral warnings. There are two conclusions: (1) God does not approve of prideful people, or of powerful rulers who disregard the lowly in their charge, or of rich people who get fat while the hungry starve; (2) God uses in special ways and looks with favor upon those of low estate. Further, the reversals are goads to lifestyle decisions and ethical action. Against any easy reduction implying that we are dealing with less than matters of eternity, recall, for example, the similar eschatological message of reversal found in the teaching of Jesus at Luke 16:19–31, a story that Helmut Gollwitzer used rather famously as the basis for a provocative book, *Rich Christians and Poor Lazarus*. That title surely causes us to take notice. The ethics of the kingdom of God lead to a certain ordering of action and values: to raise up and bless the poor, the weak, and the hungry persons among us, and to denounce and bring down those who perpetuate such hurt and disadvantage. That is work with a meaning for eternity.

There is one final point: we are reminded that God acts as God acts, according to God's covenant mercy, in history. Mary's song is a prophylactic against inappropriately spiritualizing the gospel. The Lord's work means the coming of a new heaven and a new earth. To live on earth, in history, in anticipation of its fulfillment, is the great challenge of faith.

ANDREW PURVES

PASTORAL PERSPECTIVE

The fourth Advent candle will be lit this Sunday. Some people in the congregation will have been waiting anxiously, others waiting expectantly, some waiting in deep grief, and others waiting with a threatening diagnosis received during Advent. All are waiting with memories of Christmases past, including memories of as many sermons on the Magnificat as they have experienced years in worship. The waiting is almost over. So as Mary sings her song of praise and liberation, let us listen afresh as pastoral caregivers.

In the first stanza, as we enter this expectant time with Mary and Elizabeth, we know that they both have said yes to the plan of God, which leads us to wonder what will be asked of us. Mary quickly clarifies that question as she sings that God is doing a new thing. God's Son is coming into the world and she is the bearer of God. This young Jewish girl not only accepts her calling but also sings praise to God for this amazing grace.

Then she continues her song in the second stanza, announcing how the wrongs of history will be made right. Actually, she sings as if they have *already* been made right, since she uses the past tense. Through her song of justice, Mary calls us to be change agents for a better world for all. God's call to Mary was for a specific purpose, which her cousin Elizabeth affirmed. God's call to us on this Fourth Sunday of Advent is coming to us through Mary's song. We need one another's affirmation, just as Mary needed Elizabeth's, to live into God's plan for the world. When a child is baptized, the parents vow to raise the child in the nurture and admonition of the Lord; the congregation affirms this commitment with its collective blessing and promise to support the family in this endeavor. This affirmation enables the child and the church to live into God's plan, just as Elizabeth's affirmation enabled Mary to do the same.

Looking at the poetic structure of Mary's song, we see in the second stanza seven strong verbs showing parallels or reversals: "has shown strength," "has scattered the proud," "has brought down the powerful," "[has] lifted up the lowly," "has filled the hungry," "[has] sent the rich away empty," and "has helped . . . Israel." It is important to note that God's mercy in Mary's song is described in the context of God's original covenant. "I will be your God and you will be my people." Mary's song maintains inclusion of all people in God's plan, even as her words echo both Hannah's song in 1 Samuel and the words of the prophets, preaching a strong reminder that God's purpose will always turn the status quo upside down. We can be better friends, spouses, mothers, daughters, grandmothers, and neighbors as we say yes to the new thing that God is doing with and within us.

Mary sings of the yes of God that she has learned through her Jewish faith. She knows God can be trusted, and she is therefore willing to say yes to God, even when she does not understand how a virgin like herself could bear God's Son. All of us, men and women, are included in Mary's and Elizabeth's times of expectancy, calling us together in partnership with God in God's plan for this world. This song addresses all the ways we set ourselves apart from one another, which is the excuse we need to set us over and against one another. We are all uniquely made in the image of God, meaning that we are to see God in one another and are called to say yes to justice for all.

For years Mary has been portrayed as submissive because of her yes to God at the annunciation. Today it is time to recognize that this prophetic woman also says no to all that negates God's purposes in human history. First, Mary celebrates the greatness of God, and then she proclaims God's liberating compassion for the poor. Mary sings the joy that she is feeling and sings blessing for the oppressed, whether that oppression comes from being underprivileged or overprivileged. So for the people in our pews, whatever their circumstances, Mary's new song announces the reality of "both/and." Just as she embodies the polarity of being virgin and mother, she shows us how we can be people both of the heart and of the head, both mystical and resistant, both contemplative and justice oriented, both spiritually alive and socially active.

On my first trip to the Monastery of the Holy Spirit in Conyers, Georgia, I met *Theotokos*, the God-bearer, depicted in a magnificent rose window above the altar. I was shocked by the size of Mary's womb. Mary sits in this glorious stained-glass circle with outstretched arms and a womb so large it contains Jesus standing as a grown man, with his arms open wide and enough room left over for God's rebirthing of all creation.

Every time I sit in that dark, sacred, womblike monastery sanctuary, being rocked back and forth by the sound of the monks chanting the Magnificat as evening falls, I am in awe of the *Theotokos* in the pregnant circle over the altar. The circle reminds me that Christ will come into the broken places in us and into the world where healing is needed. The circle reminds me that we are all pregnant with the possibility of new life, becoming more than we are, for God is with us and God is in us. Because our memories can be very short, we need Mary's song to remind us of God's twofold promise to deliver God's people and to lift up the poor. Mary sings because she has new life in her. Are we ready to join in singing with her? O come, let us adore him and follow him into new life.

TRISHA LYONS SENTERFITT

EXEGETICAL PERSPECTIVE

The Magnificat is one of the most famous passages in the New Testament. Mary's song, which most believe to be based on the song of Hannah in 1 Samuel 2:1–10, is one of four poems in the Bible placed in the mouths of women who play key roles in the lives of ancient Israel and Judah, those women being Miriam (Exod. 15), Deborah (Judg. 5), Hannah, and now Mary. All of these songs are placed in the narrative at key points in the history of the nation: the exodus from Egypt, formation of the nation during the period of the judges and Philistine oppression, and now Roman occupation, colonization, and oppression. All of these women are either noted in the narratives or called mother or function as substitute mothers, as in the case of Miriam and Moses at the bathing scene with Pharaoh's daughter. The men children associated with these women serve key roles in the history of the nation.

All of these songs have some relation to the liberation of the nation from oppression.[8] On the one hand, these stories and these songs are really odes to the men and the male God who empowers the men to rule. On the other hand, these songs function to reinforce the primary social role of women as mother and as comforter within the patriarchal order in which they live. As biblical scholar Cheryl Exum argues, they serve the patriarchy.[9] In terms of structure, the song has two parts, one relating to the individual (vv. 46–49) and one to the nation (vv. 50–55).

In both the vow of Hannah (1 Sam. 1:11) and the song of Mary, these women self-identify as servants, or more appropriately slaves, since verse 48 uses *doulēs*, as does LXX for 1 Samuel 1:11. This is most interesting, since both of these women come from upper-class families, as noted in the lineage of Elkanah in 1 Samuel 1:1 and Mary's priestly relatives as well as Joseph's royal background. It is as though their social class, which is prominent in the larger narratives,[10] has to be diminished by their designation as slaves of the deity. While the rich women listed in 8:2—who are reported to fund Jesus' movement—can literarily maintain their social class standing, the songs and vows of these two women must deny or misrepresent their own. While this use of *doulos* may be likened to the terminology used to describe Moses' relationship to YHWH and Paul's to God, these women are in no way equal to these men in leadership of the nation; rather they are bearers of the children who will lead/save the nation.

Scholars have long struggled against the implications of *tapeinōsin* in v. 48. As the NRSV translates this, it is "lowliness," suggesting lower social class. The word is used four times in this form in the NT. While some

---

8. Jane Schaberg, "Luke," in *The Women's Bible Commentary*, ed. Carol A. Newsom and Sharon H. Ringe (Louisville, KY: Westminster John Knox, 1998), 371–73.
9. J. Cheryl Exum, *Fragmented Women* (Valley Forge, PA: Trinity Press International, 1993), 135–39.
10. Itumeleng J. Mosala, *Biblical Hermeneutics and Black Theology in South Africa* (Grand Rapids: Eerdmans, 1989), 186–89.

suggest "humiliation" as a translation, the other usages of the term in Acts 8:33, Philippians 3:21, and James 1:10 speak to the lynching of the revolutionary by the state. *Tapeinōsin* is, however, used in LXX to speak to the oppression, exploitation, and misery of individuals, such as Hagar (Gen. 16:9), Leah (Gen. 29:32), and Hannah (1 Sam. 1:11), and of the nation by external oppressors (Deut. 26:7; 1 Sam. 9:16; and 2 Kgs. 14:26). In regard to the three women who experienced individual oppression, the reference is to the exploitation of their bodies, all with divine complicity. Some current scholarship suggests that this is the case with Mary in this passage from Luke.

In regard to the references to the national calamities, the one who comes forth is the one to lead the people in defeating these colonizers. Thus, were one to go along with "lowliness," this could not be a social-class designation as argued above. It would instead have to be a gender designation that presumes women to be worth less than men. On the one hand, this is not an unusual argument in the biblical literature, namely, that the unity of the nation or church is primary to the liberation of women from patriarchal oppression and slaves from economic exploitation. On the other hand, the term could be multivalent, speaking both to the oppression of women and slaves in the society and the Roman colonization.

In both the song of Hannah and the song of Mary, the second part of the song revolves around the theme of reversal of fortunes, namely, that the high are going to be made low and the poor are going to be raised up. The hungry will be fed, and the rich will be hungry. It is these sentiments that make these songs so powerful for those who press liberation as a major theological scheme to be found in the text. Schaberg even notes the song as paradigmatic of God's special option for those on the margins. It is this song, along with the so-called Lukan inaugural in 4:18f., that gives this Gospel its claim to being "poor friendly." Part of the difficulty with this line of argument is that nowhere in the Gospel, or in Samuel, do we find evidence of this programmatic reversal being incarnate. While these songs raise structural problems relative to social inequalities, the subsequent narratives speak more to the amelioration of the problems of individuals (as in the miracle stories) but the confrontation with the Roman Empire and its acts of colonization seems to be pushed to the background.

Finally one has to explore whether liberation of one group has to be predicated on the oppression of another group. Would not a theology of relinquishment, where those who benefit from the oppression relinquish the privileges that come from sinful social orders, serve better as a model? Or do we use such passages that have women sing in ways that support patriarchal order to model how other oppressed groups should sing about reversals that still keep them oppressed?

RANDALL C. BAILEY

HOMILETICAL PERSPECTIVE

Just when the pre-Christmas frenzy has reached its height, we are treated to the voice of the Poor One with this hymn of praise. Young Mary sings a song rooted in the legacy of her people Israel, the spiritual lineage of Miriam, and the sisterhood of Hannah, Judith, and Leah. All of them before her sang of God's reversals; but although reversal of power is one overarching scriptural mark of the Spirit's work, the Magnificat fine-tunes its paean of praise to focus upon God's handiwork in the socioeconomic arena. Here, the playing field is *more* than leveled: her stanzas envision the powerful stripped of their entitlements and the humble given preeminence. Mary speaks in two voices: for herself, initially (vv. 46b–50), although her song is anything but self-referential; and then in the third person (vv. 51–55), associating herself with all *anawim*, "handmaids" of "low estate" whom God has helped, whether by filling their barrenness or delivering Israel from its oppression.[11]

Experience indicates that the casting of Mary in the annual Christmas pageant (a nonspeaking role traditionally cast as placid and passive) can be tricky. While some little girls prefer to be angels because they *do* something, those who *want* to be Mary aspire to be the queen with royal prerogatives— an unfortunate commentary on the church's traditional interpretation of Mary's part. At the same time, we also see her as a "bit player" compared to the more energetic shepherds. But what if we restored the Magnificat to the Christmas pageant and understood Mary as a primary role model for serious disciples, bearer not only of the Savior but also of the news that God's reign has broken through our status quo?

It is a bracing focus (if also an ironic one) at the crux of a long commercial season, where all in the secular realm is focused upon acquisition and dancing to a Muzak of images angelic and snowy. At this juncture, most of us bear more resemblance to the self-satisfied than to the *anawim*. And yet those with listening ears may discern the clarion melody of a new realm in which economies are just and social injustice is undone. Preachers can help by applying Mary's template to their own communities, inviting hearers to measure their social realities by its dimensions. How do things look in "our town" today, and how *would* they look if the lowly were lifted up?

11. See Raymond E. Brown, *The Birth of the Messiah* (Garden City, NY: Image Books, 1979), 361. Note that exodus imagery predominates here as Mary describes God's acts.

The aorist verbs of Mary's canticle suggest one intriguing trajectory for preaching on the cusp of Advent, the full weight of Christmas yet to come. Scholars have long puzzled over the past tense on the lips of this pregnant young woman, who *before* giving birth speaks of her offspring's approaching mission as already accomplished—finished and done. Merely agreeing with the proposition that in her prenatal announcement Luke expresses the community's postresurrection proclamation does not fully plumb its profound depth; for this intriguing use of the past to announce a consummated future has life-changing ramifications. We might hear Mary's aorist, ultimately untranslatable in English, as a combination of anamnesis and prophecy. The first makes past history a present reality, so that we ourselves are experiencing it; the second pulls a future vision into the present. The resulting synergy reveals a vibrant *now* in which God's realm is complete and dwelling among us.

"The end is where we start from," wrote the poet. "Or say that the end precedes the beginning."[12] If so, then the saving justice of God's reign is as good as accomplished among those who can articulate its outlines. We are not used to seeing the realities around us that way. "Realists," we call ourselves—ignoring the deep implications of incarnation no less than resurrection, the new thing God has already done that sleeps below the surface of our perceptions. Our challenge is to cultivate the ability to see God's promises as already having come to pass.

Mary's words foreshadow Fred Craddock's principle that the perceptive preacher gives voice to not only what people need to *hear* but, at least occasionally, what they want to *say*. "Yes, that is it," comes the response; "that is our message; that is our faith."[13] What is it regarding divine promises fulfilled that wants articulation (and then a thankful song of praise) in your congregation or community of faith? For the preacher, the question requires seeing into the deep heart of things, to all the metaphors for liberation that even now surround us.

Can preaching offer a new set of eyes—the eyes of those perhaps *not* represented in most of our sanctuaries? How does the world look to the *anawim* of our communities? Making that vision concrete for our hearers offers them opportunity not only to look beyond the commercialism of the season but to enter a stance of *solidarity* with all whose condition was shared by Mary's child. Seeing the present world with the eyes of the poor may give

12. T. S. Eliot, *Four Quartets* (New York: Harcourt, Brace & World, 1943). The quotations are taken from "Little Gidding," stanza V, and "Burnt Norton," stanza V.
13. Fred B. Craddock, *Preaching* (Nashville: Abingdon Press, 1985), 26, 44.

us for the first time true eyes of faith to perceive the mighty acts of God now operative in the world.

The preacher should be aware that this central word of the Magnificat—that wealth and power have no ultimate influence but are brought into subservience to the lowly—will be no more a popular Christmas message in our time than it was in the culture to which Jesus' witness first came. Prepare for the possibility of ruffling some shop-weary feathers, but persist in framing the message the way Mary did: as a song of praise and the celebratory news for which all generations have been waiting!

GAIL A. RICCIUTI

Christmas Eve

²The people who walked in darkness
 have seen a great light;
those who lived in a land of deep darkness—
 on them light has shined.
³You have multiplied the nation,
 you have increased its joy;
they rejoice before you
 as with joy at the harvest,
 as people exult when dividing plunder.
⁴For the yoke of their burden,
 and the bar across their shoulders,
  the rod of their oppressor,
  you have broken as on the day of Midian.
⁵For all the boots of the tramping warriors
 and all the garments rolled in blood
  shall be burned as fuel for the fire.
⁶For a child has been born for us,
 a son given to us;
authority rests upon his shoulders;
 and he is named
Wonderful Counselor, Mighty God,
 Everlasting Father, Prince of Peace.
⁷His authority shall grow continually,
 and there shall be endless peace
for the throne of David and his kingdom.
 He will establish and uphold it
with justice and with righteousness
 from this time onward and forevermore.
The zeal of the Lord of hosts will do this.

Luke 2:1–14 (15–20)

¹In those days a decree went out from Emperor Augustus that all the world should be registered. ²This was the first registration and was taken while Quirinius was governor of Syria. ³All went to their own towns to be registered. ⁴Joseph also went from the town of Nazareth in Galilee to Judea, to the city of David called Bethlehem, because he was descended from the house and family of David. ⁵He went to be registered with Mary, to whom he was engaged and who was expecting a child. ⁶While they were there, the time came for her to deliver her child. ⁷And she gave birth to her firstborn son and wrapped him in bands of cloth, and laid him in a manger, because there was no place for them in the inn.

⁸In that region there were shepherds living in the fields, keeping watch over their flock by night. ⁹Then an angel of the Lord stood before them, and the glory of the Lord shone around them, and they were terrified. ¹⁰But the angel said to them, "Do not be afraid; for see—I am bringing you good news of great joy for all the people: ¹¹to you is born this day in the city of David a Savior, who is the Messiah, the Lord. ¹²This will be a sign for you: you will find a child wrapped in bands of cloth and lying in a manger." ¹³And suddenly there was with the angel a multitude of the heavenly host, praising God and saying,

¹⁴"Glory to God in the highest heaven,
and on earth peace among those whom he favors!"

¹⁵ When the angels had left them and gone into heaven, the shepherds said to one another, "Let's go to Bethlehem and see this thing that has happened, which the Lord has told us about."

¹⁶ So they hurried off and found Mary and Joseph, and the baby, who was lying in the manger. ¹⁷ When they had seen him, they spread the word concerning what had been told them about this child, ¹⁸ and all who heard it were amazed at what the shepherds said to them. ¹⁹ But Mary treasured up all these things and pondered them in her heart. ²⁰ The shepherds returned, glorifying and praising God for all the things they had heard and seen, which were just as they had been told.

ORDER OF WORSHIP

OPENING WORDS / CALL TO WORSHIP

Do not be afraid; for see—
I am bringing you good news of great joy.
To us is born this day in the city of David
a Savior, the Messiah, the Lord.

Luke 2:10–15

This will be a sign for you:
you will find a child wrapped in cloth
and lying in a manger.
Glory to God in the highest,
and on earth peace!

Let us go now to Bethlehem.

LIGHTING OF THE ADVENT CANDLES

[Reader 1]: We light the Christ candle to symbolize
              God's promise fulfilled.

[Reader 2]: For a child has been born for us, a son
              given to us; authority rests upon his shoulders;
              and he is named Wonderful Counselor, Mighty
              God, Everlasting Father, Prince of Peace. Glory
              to God in the highest heaven, and peace to all
              on whom his favor rests.

[All]: **Blessed be the name of the Lord.**

HYMN, SPIRITUAL, OR PSALM

CALL TO CONFESSION

In Jesus Christ our Lord
the grace of God has appeared,
bringing light to us all.
With confidence and joy,
let us confess our sin.

Isa. 9:2

PRAYER OF CONFESSION

Great and glorious God,
through Jesus Christ our Savior you have shown us
that the blessed age of grace has appeared
and the hoped-for time of salvation has come.

Yet we cling to the glories of the present age—
worldly passions and impious pursuits,
self-indulgent, crooked, and ungodly ways.
We choose to walk in darkness, *Isa. 9:2*
unwilling to see the evil your light exposes.
Cleanse us and free us;
break the yoke we choose to carry *Isa. 9:4*
through Christ, who gave himself for us,
so that we might be your people,
holy and whole. Amen.

DECLARATION OF FORGIVENESS

Hear this good news of great joy: *Luke 2:10, 14*
in Jesus Christ we are forgiven.
Thanks be to God!

Glory to God in the highest,
and peace to God's people on earth.

PRAYER OF THE DAY

Living God, on this holy night we gather— *Luke 2:1–20*
to stand with shepherds, amazed at your glory;
to sing with angels, rejoicing in your work;
to wait with Joseph, trusting in your promise;
to sit with Mary, cradling your love.
May the good news of this night inspire us
to tell the world of our great joy:
for to us is born a Savior,
the Messiah, the Lord.
Glory and praise to you forever! **Amen.**

HYMN, SPIRITUAL, OR PSALM

PRAYER FOR ILLUMINATION

Loving God, by the gift of your Spirit, *Luke 2:19*
teach us, like Mary, to treasure your words
and ponder them in our hearts;
through Jesus Christ, your Word made flesh. **Amen.**

SCRIPTURE READINGS

SERMON

HYMN, SPIRITUAL, OR PSALM

PRAYERS OF INTERCESSION
God of glory, by your grace   *Isa. 9:2–7*
a child has been born for us,
a son given to us;
authority rests on his shoulders,
and in his name we pray.

Wonderful Counselor,
we pray for wisdom for the world's leaders,
that they may use their power to lift burdens
and break the bonds of oppression.

Mighty God,
we pray for the church of Jesus Christ our Lord,
that you will multiply and increase our joy
as we share in the harvest you have gathered.

Everlasting Father,
we pray for families, friends, and loved ones,
that those who now walk in deep darkness
may see the great light of your saving love.

Prince of Peace,
we pray for an end to violence and warfare,
that your authority may continue to grow
until there is endless peace in every land.

Lord of hosts, establish your holy realm
with justice and righteousness,
from this time on and forevermore. **Amen.**

LORD'S PRAYER

INVITATION TO THE OFFERING
Rejoice at the harvest the Lord has given.   *Isa. 9:3*
Bring your first fruits with joy.
Bring honor to his name.

PRAYER OF THANKSGIVING/DEDICATION

We give you thanks, Holy One,   *Luke 2:12*
for the world of wonder you have made—
forest and field,
sea and sky,
and for the gift of grace that you have given—
a little child,
lying in a manger.
Receive these gifts of tenderness and love,
of gratitude and praise,
and use them for your glory;
in the name of Jesus Christ,
the child of Bethlehem, we pray. **Amen.**

HYMN, SPIRITUAL, OR PSALM

CHARGE

Go forth to sing and bless God's name.   *Luke 2:14*
Glory to God in the highest!
For great is the Lord, and greatly to be praised.
Alleluia! Praise the Lord.

BLESSING

The Lord look upon you with favor   *Luke 2:14*
and give you peace.

SONG SUGGESTIONS

"Angels from the Realms of Glory" (*CH* 149, *ELW* 275, *GC* 358, *GTG* 143, *TNCH* 126, *UMH* 220)

"Angels We Have Heard on High" (*CH* 155, *EH* 96, *ELW* 289, *GC* 347, *GTG* 113, *TNCH* 125)

"Hark! The Herald Angels Sing" (*CH* 150, *EH* 87, *ELW* 270, *GC* 348, *GTG* 119, *TNCH* 160, *UMH* 240)

"It Came Upon the Midnight Clear" (*CH* 153, *EH* 89–90, *ELW* 282, *GC* 367, *GTG* 123, *TNCH* 131, *UMH* 218)

"Love Has Come" (*GTG* 110)

"On Christmas Night All Christians Sing" (*ELW* 274, *GTG* 112, *TNCH* 143)

"Savior of the Nations, Come" (*ELW* 263, *GC* 334, *GTG* 102, *UMH* 214)

"Where Shepherds Lately Knelt" (*GTG* 120)

CHILDREN'S SERMON

Based on Isaiah 9:2–7

One of our Scriptures for today is from the prophet Isaiah. God chose men and women to give God's message to the people. These people were called "prophets." Isaiah was one of the most famous prophets of God. Isaiah lived about 700 years before Jesus was born. His message was for the people who lived in Judah.

When Isaiah was a prophet, countries were at war all over the place. Each king wanted power. It was a scary time for the people of Judah, and God's people were looking to kings and other human leaders for help instead of looking to God. They did not trust God, and they were not living in the ways God had shown them. They did not treat other people fairly. They were mean. And they worshiped other gods.

God's message to Isaiah for the people of Judah was a warning that their nation would be destroyed by another country's army. But the message from God also included hope. Listen for signs of hope in this part of the message God gave to Isaiah to tell the people:

"People who walked in darkness and lived in darkness will see a great light.

God will make your nation great again, and you will rejoice. You will be joyful like people having a big party with a table full of food to share!

Your burdens will be taken away, and people who want to hurt you will not bother you anymore.

For God will send us a child who is so good and powerful that he will be called Wonderful Counselor, Mighty God, Everlasting Father, Prince of Peace. He will be a good king and will reign forever and ever!"

This is also a message for people today as we celebrate how God sent us Jesus, our Prince of Peace.

Prayer: Thank you for sending us the wonderful, mighty, and everlasting Prince of Peace, Jesus Christ. Amen.

SERMON HELPS

Isaiah 9:2–7

THEOLOGICAL PERSPECTIVE

For many, Christmas Eve services are not to be missed. Music and candlelight mark the experience and the memories. Because many come to worship who are infrequently present through the movement of the liturgical year, the readings from Scripture can easily be heard in a kind of sentimental haze. Here is Isaiah again, with an astounding claim: God has come to the world in the form of a boy child born of a young woman. It is no wonder that this reading has been associated with Christmas through the centuries. It is no wonder that this reading is also heard as the culmination of prophetic desire for a Messiah. The announcement of a world-transforming reign of righteousness and justice now begun is not a sentimental set of feeling states. It is a radical prophetic claim.

As with the passage from Isaiah 7, these words are familiar to the faithful worshiper. They also contain phrases that have been planted deeply in the Western mind, whether Christian or not, by Handel's *Messiah:* "For unto us a child is born . . . a son is given." One can almost hear the music by looking at the words. The stunning messianic titles are set side by side by Handel's musical genius: "Wonderful Counselor, Mighty God, Everlasting Father, Prince of Peace." To someone on the edges of the Christian faith, this may seem impossibly hopeful, even naive. "Endless peace?" Really? "Justice with righteousness" (vv. 7a, 7b)? Where? As the world turns from one age to the next, these questions ought also to be raised by the Christmas gospel.

In order to understand what is being prophesied and sung, the promises require entering into the yearning that stands in the background of Isaiah and of all the other prophetic hopes gathered in the Christmas herald. Entering the darkness of which the opening of this passage speaks is more than coming out after dark. This is solidarity with the immense history of suffering that longs for deliverance. Such solidarity comes from having heard and known the larger pattern of biblical stories. It also comes from having become aware of the gap between the *is* of the world and God's desired *ought to be* of the world.

The power of this reading depends on our understanding something of the captivity of God's people in Babylon, yet these words speak to more than the remembered suffering of the children of Israel. Anyone held in captivity as a prisoner of war knows something of the anguish and darkness as well.

For Isaiah, the announcement of having seen a great light also speaks to those who consult their gods, their "ghosts and the familiar spirits that chirp and mutter" (8:19). When we fall back on our idols and neglect to desire and to wait in hope for God, then gloom and darkness fall upon us. Consulting our own devices and projected fantasies is itself a form of captivity.

The divine humanity in the form of the child casts light in the midst of the darkness of such human captivities. This is a light that breaks the grip of death and nothingness. To speak of light shining in the darkness is to speak of the divine persistence. In the ancient night prayer the antiphon sounded: "Jesus Christ is the Light of the world, a Light no darkness can extinguish." So this is indeed a reading that sounds the contrasts between deep darkness and the joyful light. In many Christian traditions, the symbol of the Christ candle is lit at evening prayer to the singing of the ancient Greek hymn, the *phōs hilaron* ("Hail, gladdening light").

On the eve of nativity we see how Isaiah's tense changes. What has been promised in the sign of a child is *now* to be received as gift. This *now*—figured in the prayers, hymns, and symbols of Christmas Eve—is yet paradoxically still about the future. What must have been nearly impossible for the first hearers of Isaiah's time to comprehend is here and now in this Christmas assembly equally astonishing. Given the violence of our world, with all the tramping warriors and bloody garments still reported, the gospel of a child born to Mary transforms the violence. The images of violence are themselves subverted by the child. This proclamation turns darkness into an illumination of the way of justice, peace, and righteousness. It strikes at the heart of human distress and calls out to all our captivities: "The people who walked in darkness have seen a great light" (v. 2).

What kind of sign is this that has been fulfilled? What a vulnerable sign—utterly human in its appearance, but with the power to alter human destiny! The poetic prophecy of Isaiah comingles with songs of birth and joy. This is the divine counterpoint to all human powers and principalities. Here is the wonder of divine agency at work in the midst of confusions and vagaries. Here is hope incarnate.

We look around us at the clash of nations and peoples, of the death dealing, of "ignorant armies that clash at night" and we wonder: is God aware, can God be said to act at all? To all this "nothingness," God says a definitive Word; *becomes* the definitive Word made flesh. How is this possible? Not by merely human engineering. Only by the very passion of God, as Isaiah asserts, the "zeal of the LORD of hosts" will do this. It is still to be completed. Isaiah here speaks of future events in the past tense, but this is how the eternal intention to save comes to this temporal world. That God's coming to dwell in solidarity with the human race is accomplished, means precisely that the promises will yet be so. This "Wonderful Counselor, Mighty God, Everlasting Father, Prince of Peace" is for all time and will be the light until all manner of things shall be well.

This is why we read Isaiah with the Gospel the eve of the Feast of the Nativity.

DON E. SALIERS

PASTORAL PERSPECTIVE

For many who worship on Christmas Eve the prophecy of Isaiah is inextricably connected with the celebration of Jesus' birth. Handel's *Messiah* has made it so. At first, though, this paean was for the accession of a king to the throne, quite possibly that of good King Hezekiah, in contrast to the dreaded and dreadful Ahaz.

People will grasp a political setting: Isaiah expresses the kind of hope that sometimes, but not always, accompanies new governments promising new directions for a people suffering from oppression or malaise. He sings of light overcoming darkness (v. 2), an increase of joy (v. 3), the breaking of the rod of the oppressor that would have been used to beat and subjugate the people of the land (vv. 4–5), and the promise of peace upheld with justice and righteousness (v. 7).

At Christmas a pastor may want to be aware that many people who desire change in their lives or in the world have a generalized wish that things might be different and a vague hope that they will not have to do anything but welcome the change. Many of us have a functional theology or hidden expectation that assumes an all-powerful God is supposed to fix problems. The worshiper may lapse into a spectator's passivity. Christmas Eve can be a time to refocus the celebration of Jesus' birth as the birth of one who will honor the extraordinary freedom we have been granted in creation, and whose work is not carried out by swooping in and sorting out problems for us.

It could be helpful therefore to say something about the shape of this peace Isaiah announces in the "Prince of Peace." It is God's peace, which "surpasses all understanding" (Phil. 4:7). Peace or *shalom* is that condition that becomes apparent when God is present. It cannot be other than part and parcel of a just world. Peace is dependent on right relationship or righteousness, and so is both a gift and fruit of the Holy Spirit (Gal. 5:22).[1] Right

---

1. Preachers in communities that include a passing of the peace in worship have a practice that will help anchor these contemplations of peace. One could point out that this is a prayer we offer one another as well as a recognition of the presence of God, even when we do not feel or experience it at the moment.

relationship is bound up with forgiveness, grace, and the ever-present possibility of a new start in life. The light that shines in the darkness might signal the dawn, but congregants know from experience that it does not vanquish the deep darkness all at once.

We might suggest that Søren Kierkegaard's "leap of faith" points less to the conclusion of an intellectual process beyond which there is no certainty, and more to the beginning of a journey of faith in which the content of the gift is to be filled out, explored, and understood in days and years to come as we appropriate the gift of Christmas. Faith or trust in the transforming possibilities of the newborn king is, perhaps, a gift of the season. Isaiah's paean on the accession of a king is less a celebration of the end of challenge, and more a celebration that the conditions for newness of life are upon or among us.

It can be difficult to grasp or recognize some of the ways in which God does address the reality of our lives or is present to us. Isaiah can help us come to terms with this pastoral challenge as well. Isaiah's God is concerned both with what we identify as personal matters (counselor, father) and also with societal realities (prince, governor). There is, however, no hint of coercion in any of these titles. The new government of this new king will increase without end, partly as a result of his zeal for righteousness or right relationship.

We might miss the birth of a child in a far-flung and relatively unimportant corner of an empire; we might also miss the presence or action of God nearer to hand. God will often address us obliquely or at a tangent or parabola (as in parable). Examples from the life of the preacher or preacher's community will be specific to that person or community. What they will have in common, however, is the respect of God for the freedom we are granted in creation. The word is not an indisputable word, but a Word made flesh that addresses our personal and societal situations.

Another pastoral reality to which Isaiah might speak at Christmas is the reality of abundance in a world where we are too rarely reminded of scarcity on a regular basis. Many will know the experience of the ambivalence felt on receiving a generous gift. This might attend a sense of some perceived obligation to the giver that comes with being the recipient of generosity; or maybe the experience is one of guilt at the knowledge that we have not been as generous to the one who has blessed us.

A preacher might explore the way we react to the image of the mutual joy that comes at the end of a harvest when the crop is shared (v. 3), possibly in contrast to our reactions when the boots and clothes of the warrior will be burned as fuel for the fire (v. 5). Is it possible that we could enjoy a share of abundance without jealousy, rancor, obligation, or guilt? In one perspective, it is inconceivable that the infant of Bethlehem could be sufficient for the salvation of the world. In God's perspective, however, this birth signals enough and more than enough, the possibility of unalloyed joy, rather than all of those other emotions and feelings that can so often accompany giving and receiving in our lives.

GEOFFREY M. ST. J. HOARE

EXEGETICAL PERSPECTIVE

The hopeful proclamation of the reversal of fortunes, light amid darkness, and a child's birth makes this beautiful passage a most appropriate text for the celebration of Christmas Eve. Rejoicing replaces lament, and victims become victors in the prophet's hymn of thanksgiving. This appropriateness for Christmas makes it striking that, aside from Matthew 4:15–16, which paraphrases Isaiah 9:1–2 to explain Jesus' residence in Capernaum at the beginning of his public ministry, the Gospels do not connect the Isaiah text to Jesus' nativity or messianic identity (cf. Luke 1:79). Indeed, nowhere does the NT quote or allude to the famous messianic titles (vv. 6–7) of this prophetic song. The preacher does holy work who helps a congregation imagine how this promise of a Hebrew royal birth to end Assyrian hegemony anticipates the birth of the nonroyal teaching wonder worker we celebrate on this sacred evening.

Historical Context. The book of Isaiah is attributed to Isaiah son of Amoz, who prophesied in Jerusalem during the latter half of the eighth century BCE and witnessed the rise of Neo-Assyrian imperialism. Under the aggressive policies of its king, Tiglath-pileser III (ca. 745–727 BCE), Assyria eventually conquers or annexes much of Syria and its neighbors, including the kingdom of Israel with its capital at Samaria. In opposition to the looming Assyrian presence, King Rezin of Damascus and King Pekah of Samaria form a coalition to resist the encroaching empire. They invite King Ahaz of Jerusalem to join them in imitation of successful confederacies against Assyrian aggression in the previous century. When Ahaz refuses to join their coalition, they besiege Jerusalem in order to replace him with a more malleable king, referred to as the "son of Tabeel" (Isa. 7:6). Such a puppet king is a threat not only to Ahaz, but to the entire Davidic dynasty. This conflict, called the Syro-Ephraimite War (734 BCE), is described in Isaiah 7:1–2 (cf. 2 Kgs. 16:5–9).

According to Isaiah 7:14, the prophet assures Ahaz of God's support with the sign of Immanuel. Rather than waiting on God's deliverance from the armies of Pekah and Rezin, however, Ahaz willingly submits to Tiglath-pileser III and sends him a large payment. The Assyrians then destroy Damascus (732 BCE) and annex large portions of Israel. The Assyrian deportation of Galilean populations (2 Kgs. 15:29) provides the dire context of Isaiah 9:1 and its gloomy "darkness." In this historical context, Isaiah's poem reflects a vision of renewed independence and the assurance of an unbroken line of succession for the Davidic dynasty in the aftermath of the Syro-Ephraimite War. The text may thus have been composed as a hymn in celebration of the birth of a Davidic crown prince, a coronation hymn for Hezekiah's royal inauguration, or some less specific event. Whatever the ancient social context, the text is a beautiful proclamation of a hopeful future and its vision of a just and righteous leader is timeless in its appeal.

Exegetical Remarks. Following the "gloom," "anguish," and "contempt" of 9:1, our passage begins with the powerful symbol of light shining in the darkness (v. 2). The imagery of darkness and light is common in the book of Isaiah (e.g., 2:5; 42:6; 49:6; 60:1), and later biblical writers further develop this symbolism. "Deep darkness" renders the Hebrew word *lmwt*, read as "shadow of death" in older translations of Psalm 23:4 (also Matt. 4:16 and Luke 1:79). In Hebrew poetry "the land of deep darkness" also denotes the land of the dead (Ps. 107:10–14; Job 10:21–22). In an eighth-century context, darkness symbolizes the Assyrian conquest, while light symbolizes freedom from foreign oppression.

Verse 3 addresses God directly for the first of three times (vv. 3–4) to commend what God has accomplished. The first phrase makes little sense in Hebrew, but the NRSV translation—"You have multiplied the nation"—provides a nice poetic parallel with "you have increased its joy." The people respond to God's actions by rejoicing as at harvest and dividing plunder.

Following the "light" and rejoicing of the previous two verses, verses 4–5 offer dark images of oppression, war, and bloodshed. The prophet claims that God has already broken the yoke of Assyrian oppression "as on the day of Midian," a reference to Gideon's defeat of Midian in Judges 7. The poetic parallelism of the "yoke," "bar," and "rod" of Assyria's oppression is also found in Isaiah 10:24–27. Verse 5's description of burning "all" the blood-soaked boots and garments of slain enemy soldiers is reminiscent of Ezekiel's eschatological vision of war's end in 39:9–10. Although such militaristic language of defeated enemies is unsettling, contemporary readers should appreciate the ancient writers' sense of relief and joy in freedom from warfare.

Like verses 4 and 5, verse 6 begins with the Hebrew word *kî* ("for, because") to introduce the third reason for the people's rejoicing: "For a child has been born for us." The poet speaks for the entire community to celebrate the birth of a royal heir. Scholars frequently compare the royal titles in verse 7 to ancient Egyptian throne names, and many commentators understand verse 6a as part of an enthronement ritual utilizing divine adoption language (cf. Pss. 2:7; 110:1). As royal or messianic titles, these names are not attributes of their human recipient. That is, the infant in this poem is not Mighty God and the Everlasting Father; he is named in honor of the heavenly Father. The culmination of the list in the fourth name, "Prince of Peace," answers the poem's militaristic context by offering a vision of a peaceful future.

Verse 7 describes the reign of the royal child with the hyperbolic language common to royal psalms (e.g., Ps. 89:19–37). The first phrase may originally have been a fifth throne name, but the text is not clear. Authority, peace, justice, and righteousness are explicitly linked to the throne and kingdom of David. Isaiah 11:1–5 similarly describes the righteous rule of the Davidic heir, while Psalm 72 details the royal duties of justice and integrity. The poem concludes with a final prophetic declaration: "The zeal of the Lord of hosts" will accomplish this wondrous future.

NEAL WALLS

HOMILETICAL PERSPECTIVE

Only three nights ago was the longest night of the year, the deep darkness of the winter solstice. Even if we did not know that the celebration of Christmas probably evolved from a pre-Christian solstice celebration, we could recognize that the theme of light triumphing over darkness resonates with our midwinter longings in a visceral, fundamentally human way. Our Christmas poetry and hymnody capitalize on the associations provided by elements of the natural world: the dark, cold, uncertainty, and fear of a long winter night being overcome by the light, warmth, and hope of new life and the promise of God's presence among us.

The imagery of Isaiah's oracle expands beyond light and dark, in circles eddying outward through metaphorical associations. With the shining of light comes a spirit of fecundity—the people rejoice as at the harvest. Or maybe the idea of military success is the point—and that joy over a rich harvest is replaced with the exultation of a people collecting the goods of a conquered enemy and dividing it among themselves, the victors. The imagery of warfare continues with the release experienced by captives or vassals shaking off the yoke of servitude. The idea of light overcoming darkness has been translated into liberation from slavery.

We are familiar with this series of associations, prevalent as they are in our biblical tradition and Christian poetry and hymnody. But no matter how familiar the notion of liberation from slavery may be, it is still a theme that moves even the most affluent or autonomous worshiper. There is no one, it seems, who does not feel in some sense trapped, enslaved, or limited by circumstance or personal history. This almost instinctive identification with the oppressed can sometimes be the door through which the powerful find their way to reach out to those who even now live on the margins of society. The appearance of the marginalized shepherds in the reading from Luke might offer a way to link a nativity story that is often associated with a spiritual liberation with the very literal kind of liberation celebrated by Isaiah.

Our tendency to dwell on the glory and the hope in this reading from Isaiah is encouraged by our familiarity with some of his language. It is likely that someone who has heard the reading will remember verse 6 ("For a child has been born for us . . . Wonderful Counselor, Mighty God, Everlasting Father, Prince of Peace") because the strains of Handel's *Messiah* make those words literally singable. And the words have been attached to the celebration of Christmas for so long that by now we even think of them as Christ-words rather than oracles from the Hebrew Bible. The language is familiar, hopeful, and—it would seem—Christian.

How many people, then, will remember or will even have noticed the verse immediately preceding, "For all the boots of the tramping warriors and all the garments rolled in blood shall be burned as fuel for the fire" (v. 5)? We may have been eager to associate the coming of the Messiah with liberation from oppression, or with the cosmic reversal of light out of darkness; but the imagery in this verse demands that we attend to the realities of war. The prediction of a fire fueled with warriors' boots and bloody shirts should evoke not only a vision, but the sting of oily smoke in one's eyes; rank smells of burning leather, fabric, and perhaps even flesh; heat scorching the hands and faces of those hurling wood onto the flames. It is a grisly vision.

The king celebrated in Isaiah's vision has not arrived as a savior from afar, swooping in and rescuing people from slavery. This messiah has been a leader of warriors, overcoming the strength of the oppressors with the sword. The king mounts his throne stepping over the bodies of those—from both sides—sacrificed for his victory.

What if we stopped for just a moment to recall these grim details of Isaiah's messianic oracle, before embracing the happier prediction of the child to be born? What if we stopped for just a moment to take in the fact that the glorious throne of David was steeped in blood? Indeed, most of the rulers celebrated in biblical history secured their power through ruthless oppression of their enemies. And in that moment we recognize as "the fullness of time" (Gal. 4:4), the people of Israel were suffering under a succession of violent puppet kings who sold them to the domination of a foreign empire. How might an honest reflection on the violence and death that marked the stories of the kings color our understanding of the nativity we await, and the incarnation we celebrate?

This passage from Isaiah challenges us to push a few inches beyond the comfortable picture of the nativity tableau. The child whose birth we attend tonight was born into a world painted not in pastels but in dust and blood. This incarnation is not a spiritual, otherworldly concept, but the mystery of God present in a real human child, welcomed into a real world with all its agonies and ambiguities and challenges and joys.

Once we have reconnected with the earthiness of Isaiah's vision, we can step away again to the wider perspective of the prophet, who is fundamentally singing of the zeal and the steadfastness of YHWH. The people who have suffered persecution and been liberated are the people to whom the Lord has declared eternal faithfulness. The king who is announced in these verses is a king chosen and elevated by the God of Jacob. And the peace, justice, and righteousness with which the king will establish rule are gifts of the Lord of hosts. Our celebration tonight invites us to wonder at the mystery of this cosmic creative power, steadfast love, and irrepressible force for justice embodied in the fragile flesh of a newborn child.

LINDA LEE CLADER

Luke 2:1–14

THEOLOGICAL PERSPECTIVE

In the wonderful play *The Best Christmas Pageant Ever*, a family of poor kids—aptly named Herdman—hijack a children's Christmas pageant, taking all the choice roles by intimidation and force. As the performance degenerates into chaos, the youngest Herdman, who plays the angel announcing the Messiah's birth to the shepherds, yells out over the din, "Hey! Unto you a child is born!" Thankfully, the great good news of Jesus' birth, the event of the incarnation, can still cut through the noise of our distracted culture and our own restless souls.

At least three incarnational themes have roots in this passage: its historical location, its spiritual location, and its social location.

1. The manger of Bethlehem indicates the *historical location* of the incarnation. The names of Caesar and Quirinius reveal Luke's historical consciousness. God entered human history as a baby boy born to Mary in Bethlehem. "For in him all the fullness of God was pleased to dwell" (Col.

1:19). Philosophers and religious thinkers over the years have stumbled over the "scandal of particularity," God locating himself in human history as Jesus. Modern humanity seems to expect that if God reveals himself at all (a big "if"), then God is revealed in universal truths and principles, and not particularly in space and time in history. The older philosophers expressed it this way: the finite is not capable of the infinite (*finitus non capax infiniti*). As Lessing put it, "the accidental truths of history can never become the proof of necessary truths of reason."[2] On this view, one "marginal Jew" living in the first century CE in a backwater province of the Roman Empire could not possibly be the full and complete revelation of God.

The manger of Bethlehem is God's counterargument: this decisive act of revelation and reconciliation was not an announcement of universal principles or truths; instead it was a baby. The manger shouts back that God is capable of dwelling among his people. The first baby steps of the infant Jesus were the fulfillment of the age-old covenant promise: "And I will walk among you, and will be your God, and you shall be my people" (Lev. 26:12).

2. The celebration of the angels indicates the *spiritual location* of the incarnation. The Bethlehem manger is the divinely appointed intersection of heavenly and earthly realms that brings peace on earth and fosters goodwill among mortals. The angels bear witness to this when they declare peace on earth, an end to the estrangement between God and humanity. Gregory the Great noted: "Because the King of heaven has taken unto himself the flesh of our earth, the angels from their heavenly height no longer look down on our infirmity. Now they are at peace with us, putting away the remembrance of the ancient discord."[3]

In Luke's account, angels bear witness to the event of the incarnation. As God enters space and time, so the hosts of the heavenly realm break into the earthly realm to announce the incarnation. Interestingly, the angels participate only indirectly in the event by foretelling its coming (Luke 1) or announcing its happening (Luke 2). Given the widespread interest in angels in popular culture, Christians need to be reminded that angels point only to Christ and his ongoing ministry of revelation and reconciliation, and not to themselves.

3. The announcement to the shepherds indicates the *social location* of the incarnation. One might expect the Son of God to be born in more

---

2. G. E. Lessing, *On the Proof of Spirit and Power*, quoted in Alistair McGrath, ed., *The Christian Theology Reader*, 3rd ed. (Oxford: Blackwell, 2007), 296.
3. Gregory the Great, *Homilies on the Gospels* 8.2, quoted in Arthur A. Just Jr., ed., *Luke*, Ancient Christian Commentary on Scripture: New Testament 3 (Downers Grove, IL: InterVarsity, 2003), 42.

dignified surroundings and celebrated by more upscale admirers. In the first of many "great reversals," God bypasses the proud and the powerful (Luke 1:51–52) in favor of a stable surrounded by livestock and visited by lowly shepherds—"not . . . enfolded in Tyrian purple, but . . . wrapped with rough pieces of cloth . . . not . . . in an ornate golden bed, but in a manger." Bede quotes from 2 Corinthians, "Though he was rich, yet for our sake he became poor, so that by his poverty we might become rich."[4]

While it is clear that Christ came to be Savior for all persons, rich and poor alike, it is also equally clear that God chose to dwell among the least and the lost. Shepherds had little status and did menial work for low pay. Yet God has "lifted up the lowly" (Luke 1:52) by making humble shepherds the first to visit him. Thus the Savior spent his first hours surrounded by the lost ones whom he came to seek and save (Luke 19:10). Jesus' later practices underscored the earthiness of the incarnation as he chose to be with the poor, the marginalized, and the outcast.

This social location of the incarnation continues to challenge our notions of who is blessed by God: "on earth peace among those he favors" (v. 14). The favor of God—the grace of God—comes not to those who think they've earned it by birth or education or success in the world. The grace of God sneaks into our world under the radar of our religious expectations, in the person of Jesus. The "good news" the angels proclaimed turns out to be better than we thought or dared to dream, for it offers the promise of peace with God and the favor of God through him who is the Savior on the basis of his love and covenant faithfulness. In welcoming the announcement of Jesus' birth, we too can treasure and ponder in our hearts what Mary treasured and pondered in hers.

In the words of Phillips Brooks, "O holy Child of Bethlehem, descend to us we pray / Cast out our sin and enter in, be born in us today. / We hear the Christmas angels the great glad tidings tell. / O come to us, abide with us, Our Lord Emmanuel."

ROBERT REDMAN

PASTORAL PERSPECTIVE

A couple that was planning to adopt a child of another race was told by their social worker that they would become what is known as a "conspicuous family." This term was coined to prepare prospective parents to be the object of others' attention in public places. Intended to be helpful, the description is

---

4. Bede, *Exposition of the Gospel of Luke 1*, quoted in Just, *Luke*, 38–39.

sometimes met with resistance because it highlights difference as an obstacle, instead of coaxing the culture to be more accepting.

Luke's account of Jesus' birth suggests that Mary and Joseph were *not* conspicuous when they went to Jerusalem to register for the census. The passage makes no note of anyone going out of the way to accommodate this young couple that was a long way from home, wearied by travel, and probably visibly preoccupied with the impending birth of their baby. Christmas pageant scripts sometimes embellish the plot by assigning curt lines to an officious innkeeper whose hotel is full, but the text presents that aspect of the story almost as an afterthought, including it as a way of explaining why this young mother placed her newborn son in a manger instead of the more traditional and comfortable cradle.

Church school pageant directors are also inclined to incorporate farm animals into the story, but there is no reference to them in the actual text. While a stable is often presumed, the location of the manger is unspecified. In fact, nothing in verses 1–7 suggests that Jesus' birth was noteworthy. Quietly Mary and Joseph go about their business as good citizens and expectant parents. When Jesus is delivered, no midwife is mentioned, nor does the passage name anyone else who was present in the unspecified setting where the manger was located. Despite the secluded location where Jesus was born, word of his arrival quickly gets out! Before the orange of dawn pales the sky, the new parents find themselves greeting strangers: shepherds who show up in grimy work clothes, summoned from the fields by angels who serenaded them with news of the triply superlative birth of an infant who was Savior, Messiah, and Lord, born in the city of David. Although the angel Gabriel had informed Mary that her child would be the Son of God, it is doubtful that a social worker had primed her and Joseph for the unprecedented attention they received on the night Jesus was born. At that moment, Mary, Joseph, and Jesus must have felt as if they were a conspicuous family. Persons who prefer anonymity will relate to this experience by observing that Mary and Joseph may have desired privacy in their first hours of parenthood.

Many pastors have heard ironic regret expressed by active church members who indicate that they will not be in attendance on Christmas Eve because the timing conflicts with their family gatherings. Among those whose circumstances are conducive to worshiping on Christmas Eve are childless adults who are not granted sufficient time off from work to journey to see relatives, or others whose financial situations prevent them from doing so, as well as elderly individuals who do not feel up to traveling. In other words, those whose sparse schedules and geographic isolation from their families facilitates their availability to worship on Christmas Eve may be individuals who do not receive an excess of adoration or attention. Like the shepherds who lived outside the mainstream of society, these devoted churchgoers may feel overlooked by the world. For that very reason, they just may be the ones who are most deeply touched by the angels' announcement and the shepherds' contagious amazement. According to the angel's song, the Messiah's birth conveys goodwill. No one is inconspicuous in the eyes of the savior. Therefore, in this case, the special attention is positive. Jesus' birth carries peace to those whom he favors. This pastoral word can compel households that once echoed with emptiness to resound with incomparable joy!

For centuries, the country from which one's ancestors emigrated was emphasized and often influenced one's social station in the United States. In many communities, lineage still extends security to some residents, and erects hurdles that others struggle to overcome. Prejudice toward persons of particular ethnicities continues. At the same time, many ache to be associated with a people or in tune with a culture. Joseph's lineage was a critical factor in the events that unfolded. Because the governmental decree mandated that he return to his native city, he and his betrothed were far from home when their firstborn son entered the world. Like Mary and Joseph, many new parents today are also separated from their families of origin and experience the momentous occasion of birth without relatives there to provide support in person. And the nomadic tendency rarely ends at that juncture. Few children graduate from high school in the town indicated on their birth certificate. Joseph's return to his hometown affirms the importance of feeling connected to a place, as well as the inconvenience of it. A word of empathy arises for those who feel adrift or displaced from their roots.

The woe attached to a mobile society that scatters close relatives across the continent exists in tandem with a blessing. Unlikely acquaintances become intimately involved in one another's lives. Local churches frequently find themselves innately adept at facilitating these essential relationships, as they pray for and with one another and share meals together. Amid a populace that exhibits tentative hospitality toward atypical families, congregations celebrate the Lord's Supper, a sacrament that models what it means to be welcoming. The inclusive Communion table invites and accepts persons of disparate backgrounds, illustrating the value of a broadened sense of family and making the church a "conspicuous family" in a world that is inclined to judge the stranger and exclude the other.

When their son was born, Mary and Joseph were away from their immediate families, yet shepherds with whom they may have thought they had little in common were present to share their immeasurable gladness. On

Christmas Eve, some people have the privilege of spending time with their blood relatives, and all are embraced by the glorious news of peace and goodwill.

ASHLEY COOK CLEERE

EXEGETICAL PERSPECTIVE

This reading provides the Christmas tableau of baby Jesus in the manger and of shepherds watching their flocks by night, who receive the heavenly Christmas proclamation: "there is born to you today a savior in the city of David, Christ the Lord" (v. 11, my trans.). This passage is the culmination of the preceding narratives about the births of Jesus and John. It concludes with the shepherds spreading the news, "proclaiming all they had seen or heard" (v. 20) and so, with Mary (v. 19), becoming links in a series of human witnesses transmitting the heavenly witness of the angelic host (for its extension, see Acts 1:8). Heaven and earth pause for a moment in awe, with audible wonder, joy, and praise at what God has wrought.

Luke opens this part of his extended introductory section by dating the events, like a Greek and Roman historian, by the reigning emperor and local Roman ruler: Jesus was born amid a general census under Augustus Caesar (v. 1) and during the office of the imperial legate in Syria, Quirinius (v. 2). But the calendar math does not work well. The general phrase "in these days" of verse 1 seems to refer back to "the days of King Herod of Judah" (1:5), who died in 4 BCE. This is difficult to reconcile with the dates for the office holding of Publius Sulpicius Quirinius, appointed governor of Syria in 6 CE and charged to conduct a census in Syria and Palestine. Also, despite smaller censuses under Augustus, nothing suggests he ever ordered a universal census (as Luke in 2:1 states). Finally, enrollments in censuses and registrations of property were done in the place of residence, not the place of birth.[5]

Whatever the extent of Luke's familiarity with these political events, one narrative function for the sentence is to bring Jesus' parents out of their hometown, Nazareth in Galilee (v. 4), and into Bethlehem of Judah. Although Luke does not refer to the specific prophecy (Mic. 5:2) that Matthew employs to anchor the birth of the Messiah in Bethlehem (Matt. 2:6), he does present Jesus, the son of Joseph who is "from the house and hometown of David" (v. 4; 1 Sam. 16:1), as having the requisite messianic ancestry. A second narrative function may be to imply an oppressive political setting,

---

5. See a full discussion in C. F. Evans, *Saint Luke*, TPI New Testament Commentaries (London: SCM Press, 1990), 190–97.

in which self-involved rulers can move subjects around their map like pawns on a chessboard (see 2 Sam. 24 and Ps. 87:6).

Both the means of dating and the travel itinerary serve to frame the spectacle Luke creates of wonder and joy fitting the occasion of the savior's birth. The manger, the vulnerability of the setting of the birth, and the resourcelessness of his parents to secure better lodgings (2:7) all mirror the vulnerabilities of subjugated peoples like Jews (3:12–14) and marginalized groups like early Christians (21:12–19) to local and imperial rulers. Yet the humble setting puts no damper on the joyous event. The Christmas joy of the birth story and the "joy" of the resurrection news at the end of the gospel (24:41, 52) frame the largely somber tone of the Gospel and the dolorous passion narrative.

Luke presents Jesus' birth as the birth also of a message, the good news of the gospel. The implications of what is being revealed—what is inside the wrapping—are indicated in Jesus' first sermon in a Nazareth synagogue and made fully manifest at the Gospel's conclusion (4:14–21; 24:46–49), but are here expressed summarily by the angel announcing to the shepherds "news of great joy for all the people: to you is born this day . . . a Savior" (v. 11). That Jesus is specified as Mary's "firstborn son" (v. 7) serves not only to sustain the earlier statement of her virginity (1:27) but also to highlight the status of the firstborn son as particularly beloved to women, who in the patriarchal culture were under pressure to produce male offspring (see Gen. 30:1–4).

The details of the narrative focus the reader's attention on a moment in time and space. The "great joy" (v. 10) of the proclamation of the savior's birth greets this opening of heaven to earth, a motif communicated through a double and intensified vision, first of "the glory of the Lord" (v. 9) and then of "a multitude of the heavenly host" (v. 13). This latter vision is of angelic worship and praise of God in the words that epitomize the Christmas message: "Glory to God in the highest heaven and on earth peace among those of God's favor!" (v. 14). God inclines to people drawn by the weight of the divine love: peace—fulfillment, not a mere absence of strife—is love's gift.

This meeting of heaven and earth, as Luke conceives it, does not presuppose any infusion of a divine substance into an earthly vehicle—such as some interpretations of the Johannine prologue might suggest—but the fulfillment of a divine intention for human salvation, much as was the baby born as a sign in Isaiah 7:13–16 (v. 17 is not part of the original oracle). Luke's understanding of the virgin birth of the Messiah does not suppose any theory of incarnation, but works with a "chosen one" Christology (see the speeches in Acts, e.g., 2:22, 36; 5:31).

The final verses of the reading (vv. 15–20) narrate the shepherds' going to Bethlehem, seeing the scene, relating the angelic message, and at their departure witnessing to "all they had seen and heard just as it was told to them" (v. 20). These verses are dominated by terms of hearing, seeing, speaking—or being told—and other forms of declaring. This fits the basic sense of the passage as about revelation and witness, about a movement from heaven to earth and the spread of that movement on earth. That horizontal movement for Luke extends "to the ends of the earth" (Acts 1:8), but the night on which it begins, when time stops in that very specific humble stable, a new thing of God is born.

STEPHEN A. COOPER

HOMILETICAL PERSPECTIVE

On Christmas Eve, the fulfillment of a long wait is realized, as "Come, Thou Long-Expected Jesus" gives way to "Joy to the World." At the beginning of Advent, the world aches for a Messiah; now those who walked in darkness see a great light, for a child is born (see Isa. 9:2–7). Christmas is not merely an anniversary celebration of Jesus' birth—that is, it is not just the marking of an event in history—but the active remembering of what God has already accomplished in Jesus Christ and the promise of the coming completion of God's reign. At Christmas we proclaim not only the birth of Jesus, but the birth of the new creation (see Rev. 21). Despite what the newspapers seem to say every day, the way has been made clear; the chasm between God and humanity has been bridged because of the birth of Christ, and God's reign of justice and peace has already begun.

The vivid narratives of Christmas help us remember this actively, as is seen in the Gospel lesson recommended for Christmas Eve. What a story! The divine breaks in once again, this time in the form of a whole host of angels. And once again the natural response is fear. This should come as no surprise by now—Zechariah and Mary reacted this way, too. The angels' words are always the same: do not be afraid. But perhaps the preacher would do well to recapture that sense of fear of the divine—not a cowering before some malevolent spirit, but an awe before that which (or Whom) is far beyond our comprehension or knowledge, greater than our fragile, flawed, and mortal selves.

The main human actors in this narrative are the shepherds, of course. They seem unlikely messengers, until we take note of Luke's reminders that Joseph is a descendant of the house of David—David, the quintessential shepherd-king. This newborn son of David is born the ultimate shepherd-king, and an unlikely Messiah. These shepherds are hardly the ones we would expect to be entrusted with such earth-changing news, and yet they are the ones who are led to his birthing place, the ones who leave rejoicing and telling the good news to everyone they meet.

Shepherds were held in low esteem in those days; they lived outside the boundaries of polite society, were assumed to lead shiftless lives, and would hardly be considered trustworthy sources for any news of import. And yet they are the first to hear, the first to see, the first to tell of Jesus' birth. Paul indicates that this is God's way, as he writes to Christians in Corinth:

> Consider your own call, brothers and sisters: not many of you were wise by human standards, not many were powerful, not many were of noble birth. But God chose what is foolish in the world to shame the wise; God chose what is weak in the world to shame the strong; God chose what is low and despised in the world, things that are not, to reduce to nothing things that are. (1 Cor. 1:26–28)

This theme is reflected over and over in the Lukan Christmas narrative: in the annunciation to Mary, in her Magnificat, in the mean circumstances of Jesus' birth, in the calling of the shepherds to see and tell. Reflecting on these words of Paul's from 1 Corinthians, Nora Gallagher writes, "What if those words are about something real? What if they are a hint about the kingdom? A hint about God? What if this religion I've been practicing and this Gospel . . . I've heard from the priest every Sunday, is not a metaphor but a description of reality?"[6] To ask this question is to take a deep look into the meaning of the birth of Christ, the possibility that gospel truth is found today in the lives and witness of people we would not see as strong or powerful. Preachers might do well to remind listeners of this element of the Christmas story in the midst of a culture that puts great stock in following the ways of the influential, the good-looking, and the wealthy.

What does it mean to proclaim that Christ was born in a barn? The preacher dares not romanticize this birth story. Finding the Messiah in such impoverished circumstances was as amazing then as it would be now. Would we believe it if we were led to a newborn Savior in a homeless shelter or a truck stop? But here it is, in Luke's story: the Savior of the world, the Word incarnate, takes on human flesh in the most ordinary way.

Those preachers who seek to lead worshipers to the eucharistic table on Christmas Eve might look to the manger itself. Luke mentions the manger three times, pointing to its significance.[7] That the shepherds greet God

6. Nora Gallagher, *Things Seen and Unseen: A Year Lived in Faith* (New York: Alfred A. Knopf, 1998), 73.
7. Robert C. Tannehill, *Luke* (Nashville: Abingdon Press, 1996), 65.

incarnate not only in a barn but in the animals' trough points us to the table—Luke does not show Jesus resting on a pile of quilts in the corner, but in the feeding place. This baby, resting in a manger on the night of his birth, will be "the bread of God . . . which comes down from heaven and gives life to the world," the very "bread of life" (John 6:33, 35). Each time the community gathers around the table, it remembers this mystery: that though it is beyond our comprehension, God took on human form, lived among us, suffered for us, died and was raised, that we might know true life, in this world and the next. How fitting, then, that the church celebrates the Lord's Supper on Christmas, remembering how God became one of us, remembering how Christ still joins us at the Table, remembering how we are fed by him in order that we might live as his body in the world. It is a mystery indeed that we celebrate on Christmas Eve, one that reaches beyond even what Luke can tell us. The birth of Jesus is an incomprehensible inbreaking of the holy, as is his presence with us at the Table, and each and every day—a mystery for which we can respond only with our thanks and praise.

KIMBERLY BRACKEN LONG

Christmas Day

Isaiah 52:7–10

⁷How beautiful upon the mountains
    are the feet of the messenger who announces peace,
who brings good news,
    who announces salvation,
    who says to Zion, "Your God reigns."
⁸Listen! Your sentinels lift up their voices,
    together they sing for joy;
for in plain sight they see
    the return of the LORD to Zion.
⁹Break forth together into singing,
    you ruins of Jerusalem;
for the LORD has comforted his people,
    he has redeemed Jerusalem.
¹⁰The LORD has bared his holy arm
    before the eyes of all the nations;
and all the ends of the earth shall see
    the salvation of our God.

John 1:1–14

¹In the beginning was the Word, and the Word was with God, and the Word was God. ²He was in the beginning with God. ³All things came into being through him, and without him not one thing came into being. What has come into being ⁴in him was life, and the life was the light of all people. ⁵The light shines in the darkness, and the darkness did not overcome it.

⁶There was a man sent from God, whose name was John. ⁷He came as a witness to testify to the light, so that all might believe through him. ⁸He himself was not the light, but he came to testify to the light. ⁹The true light, which enlightens everyone, was coming into the world.

¹⁰He was in the world, and the world came into being through him; yet the world did not know him. ¹¹He came to what was his own, and his own people did not accept him. ¹²But to all who received him, who believed in

his name, he gave power to become children of God, [13]who were born, not of blood or of the will of the flesh or of the will of man, but of God.

[14]And the Word became flesh and lived among us, and we have seen his glory, the glory as of a father's only son, full of grace and truth.

ORDER OF WORSHIP

OPENING WORDS / CALL TO WORSHIP

Christ is born!
Alleluia!
Jesus is among us!
Alleluia!
The Word has become flesh!   *John 1:14*
Alleluia! Alleluia!

LIGHTING OF THE ADVENT CANDLES

[Reader 1]: We light these candles once again in celebration of the light of life, now with us forevermore.

[Reader 2]: For the Word has become flesh and is dwelling among us. We have seen his glory, the glory as of a father's only son, full of grace and truth.

[All]: **Glory to God. Amen.**

HYMN, SPIRITUAL, OR PSALM

CALL TO CONFESSION

Even on this day of celebration,
let us come before the Holy One of Israel
confessing our sins with contrite hearts,
so that we may not deceive ourselves,
but instead know the truth of our forgiveness.

PRAYER OF CONFESSION

Almighty God,
we confess that our hearts have not been open
to all that you have revealed to us in the nativity of your Son.

You sent Christ to be born as a helpless Child,
and yet we have not attended to suffering
of children.
You chose humble Mary to be mother of
our Lord Jesus,
and yet we have not attended to the struggles
of women.
The holy family could find no room in Bethlehem
but a stable,
and yet we have not attended to the cry of
the homeless.
You announced your birth to lowly shepherds,
yet we ignore those who tend our farms and fields.
Forgive our lack of attention,
and free us for joyful compassion,
that we may know Christ in serving others.
Through Jesus Christ we pray. Amen.

DECLARATION OF FORGIVENESS

Break forth into singing,   *Isa. 52:7–10*
for the Lord has redeemed you.
See the salvation of God;
find comfort in his strong arms.

PRAYER OF THE DAY

On this day, Gracious Lord, you come to us as Word,
    as light, as flesh.   *John 1:4–5*
Teach us to know you so well
that our lives may befriend this world you have made,
in the name of the Holy Trinity: Father, Son, and
    Holy Spirit,   *John 1:1–2*
one God, now and forever. **Amen.**

HYMN, SPIRITUAL, OR PSALM

PRAYER FOR ILLUMINATION

By the light of the Holy Spirit shining in our midst, *John 1:5*
open our hearts and minds, O God, to your Word,
present now and always for the sake of your
    holy name. **Amen.**

SCRIPTURE READINGS

SERMON

HYMN, SPIRITUAL, OR PSALM

PRAYERS OF INTERCESSION
[A time of silence may follow each petition.]
Let us pray for the world in which the
    Prince of Peace took flesh
and form, saying,
hear us, O God; your mercy is great.

We give you thanks, Holy One,
for the light that has come into the darkness
    of our world,   *John 1:3–5, 9*
for the truth illuminated,
for the pathway that has opened,
for the rejoicing of your people.
Hear us, O God; **your mercy is great.**

We give you thanks for the feet of those
who bring good news, friendship, comfort,   *Isa. 52:7*
food, shelter, and medicine for healing.
Hear us, O God; **your mercy is great.**

We give you thanks for the church of Christ Jesus
and for all people of faith
whose attention to the way of peace
tears down walls that keep us apart.
Hear us, O God; **your mercy is great.**

We give you thanks for this country
and for every nation where wisdom reigns,
where leaders work for the well-being of the poor,
so that no one is hungry or homeless,
and every child is valued and nourished.
Hear us, O God; **your mercy is great.**

We pray for the knowledge and courage
to be good stewards of all that you have given us:
ourselves, our neighbors, the strangers among us,
the oceans and rivers, the air and soil,
creatures large and small,
that we may continue to be blessed with health and life.
Hear us, O God; **your mercy is great.**

We pray for those whose flesh is harmed
by poverty, sickness, and cruelty of any kind,
that the Word-made-flesh may so fill your world   *John 1:14*
with the power to heal
that all people would be made strong and whole.
Hear us, O God; **your mercy is great.**

We pray for those concerns yet unnamed this day . . .
[A time of silence is kept to allow for responses.]
Hear us, O God; **your mercy is great.**

We commend all these things to you
and offer our thanksgiving,
trusting that what we have left unsaid,
your holy wisdom can unearth;
in the name of the One who came among us
in the power of the Holy Spirit, one God,
　　now and forever. **Amen.**

LORD'S PRAYER

INVITATION TO THE OFFERING
For the sake of those in need,
for the care of the church in proclaiming Christ's birth,
and for all that God calls us to do,
let us gather our tithes and offerings.

PRAYER OF THANKSGIVING/DEDICATION
On this glad new day for all the earth
we are grateful for giving hearts made joyful
in the gift of your Son.
For you, O God, are generosity itself.

Bless these gifts we offer to the benefit of those in need.
Bless our lives in service of sharing your love
    in the world;
through Jesus Christ we pray. **Amen.**

HYMN, SPIRITUAL, OR PSALM

CHARGE
God's Word has come to earth to bring us
    together in love.   *John 1:1–14*
Go in peace to love and serve Christ.
    Alleluia, alleluia!
Thanks be to God. Alleluia, alleluia!

BLESSING
Now may the true light shine on you.   *John 1:9*
May the Son sent by God be your guide
    and strength.
May you go in peace and live in hope,
in Jesus' name.

SONG SUGGESTIONS

"Awake! Awake, and Greet the New Morn" (*CH* 138, *ELW* 242, *GC* 346, *GTG* 107, *TNCH* 107)

"Break Forth, O Beauteous Heavenly Light" (*GTG* 130, *TNCH* 140, *UMH* 184)

"Jesus, Jesus, O What a Wonderful Child" (*ELW* 297, *GTG* 126, *TNCH* 136)

"Joy to the World" (*CH* 143, *EH* 100, *ELW* 267, *GC* 341, *GTG* 134, *TNCH* 132, *UMH* 246)

"O Come, All Ye Faithful" (*CH* 148, *EH* 83, *ELW* 283, *GC* 341, *GTG* 133, *TNCH* 135, *UMH* 234)

"Of the Father's Love Begotten" (*CH* 104, *EH* 82, *GTG* 108, *TNCH* 118, *UMH* 184)

"Raise a Song of Gladness" (*GTG* 155)

CHILDREN'S SERMON

Based on John 1:1–9

This writer—let's call him John—was thinking deeply. He wanted to find a way to tell people about Jesus so that people would understand what a special person Jesus was. He wanted to tell about Jesus in such a way that people would say, "Wow, Jesus is amazing!" He wanted to tell Jesus' story from the very beginning.

So he wrote, "In the beginning was Jesus. Jesus was with God. Jesus was God. Jesus was with God in the beginning."

The writer thought some more. "This is hard," he said, scratching his head.

Then he wrote, "Everything was created by Jesus and God. God and Jesus gave life to everything that was created. The life was light for all the world, and all the people in the world."

"Ah, light!" He had new energy for writing now. "Jesus is that light. The light of Jesus came into the darkness, and nothing could put that light out. John the Baptist told everyone to believe in the light of Jesus. Some people didn't believe, but those who did believe welcomed the light of Jesus."

The writer stopped and read what he had written. Then he added, "Jesus came to earth looking just like an ordinary person. He lived among ordinary people too. Now we have seen his glory, like the glory of God, full of grace and truth."

With that, the writer leaned back. Yes, he thought, this will help people understand how special Jesus is.

Prayer: Thank you, God, for writers who have passed down the story of Jesus so that we can hear it again today. Amen.

SERMON HELPS

Isaiah 52:7–10

THEOLOGICAL PERSPECTIVE

Coming at the end of another long passage from Second Isaiah's proclamation of good news for Zion in exile (51:1–52:12), Isaiah 52:7–10 both describes the reason for that good news and signals its magnitude.

The reason is that after a long exile, God's sleeves are rolled up and God is taking action in the world. By his bared holy arm he has redeemed Jerusalem and established justice. For Second Isaiah, then, the historic events leading up to the return from exile ought to be interpreted within the context of divine activity. (For this reason, incidentally, we need not settle the question of whether Second Isaiah's regular use of the image of God's "arm" should be interpreted as synecdoche for the divine being or as metaphor for a human agent: synecdoche and metaphor theologically collapse into each other when historic events—including human actions—are interpreted as driven by divine action.)

The claim that God is working in and shaping world events is fraught with implication for how we think about God. On the one hand, it is cause for rejoicing: We are not left exposed to the whims of history, because history neither tells nor shapes itself. Nor are we left to the caprice of the powerful, because they control neither our destinies nor their own. On the other hand, such a claim compels us to ask questions about the mysterious and dangerous ways this God works: the same God who delivers the exiles participated in carrying them off. Following theologically on First Isaiah's heels, Second Isaiah offers no vision of a beneficent (if removed) God who occasionally steps in to do good things. Instead, this God is powerful and intimately connected to all that happens—one who follows exiling with restoring. In such a theology, the incarnation would not be about God stepping into human history from the outside so much as God becoming flesh as a new way of acting in that history.

The claim is also fraught with implication in how we think about salvation. For Second Isaiah, God's activity in the midst of historic events means that the good news of salvation is neither a rapturous spiritual escape from the world (as if body and soul could be divided) nor a stoic mental escape from it (as if body and mind could be divided). The nature of the good news of salvation is that it does not demand that the exiles excise part of themselves to benefit from it. As Christians celebrate the incarnation of a Messiah today, it is wise to remember this: salvation is integrative, not divisive. That, in itself, ought to be a source of comfort and celebration.

How extraordinary is this good news? It is so good that the exiles rejoice even before it is achieved. They praise the very feet of the messenger who is bringing news to Zion that its citizens are on their way home; they break into singing when the sentinels send out word that the exiles can be seen in the distance; they are comforted even before they celebrate their reunions. The salvation they celebrate is so good that they need not feel its full impact to begin offering praise. Even the verb tenses in the passage play up the relationship between what has already happened, what is happening, and what has yet to happen, moving constantly between perfect tense ("has comforted," "has redeemed," "has bared"), present tense ("reigns," "see"), and future tense ("shall see," "will go before you").

This temporal tension sits at the theological heart of this passage. It sits at the heart of the Christian faith as well. In Advent, we waited for the God who came to us in the form of a manger-born baby, and we wait for God to come again. At Easter, we celebrate Jesus' resurrection, and await the second resurrection. Daily, we rejoice in creation, and, as Paul writes, we groan in labor pains for the new creation (Rom. 8:18ff.). Picking up on this tension, John Calvin wrote of this passage, "The Lord hath changed the mourning of the people into joy, and out of captivity hath made them free. Yet some person will say that this has not yet happened. But in the promises of God, as in a mirror, we ought to behold those things which are not yet visible to our eyes, even though they appear to us to be contrary to reason."[1]

Most of us are academically and existentially familiar with living between what God has done and what God will do. But how peculiar to highlight that tension on Christmas Day! Weeks of Advent waiting end with this day; some type of celebration at the culmination of the last four-plus weeks would seemingly make more sense than to be told that our waiting is not over. Today is about a newborn, not a pregnancy.

Perhaps, though, this is a particularly appropriate text for Christmas Day, for it serves to remind us of two things. First, Christmas (and for that matter, all of our holidays) are not points of temporal conclusion but proleptic participants in a time when all things reach their consummation: to use Calvin's metaphor, the joys we feel here are reflections as in a mirror of what will be when God's promises are ultimately fulfilled. As magnificent as it is, the incarnate presence of God with us only hints at that time when we are present with God. Second, our response to living between "the already" and "the not yet" is neither quietism nor anxiety; instead, it is gratitude and praise. As we learn to see even the feet of the messenger as praiseworthy, we gain practice in praise for that day when the ends of the earth do see the salvation of our God and praise is all that is left to do.

MARK DOUGLAS

---

1. John Calvin, *Commentary on the Book of Isaiah*, trans. William Pringle, in *Calvin's Commentaries*, 22 vols. (Grand Rapids: Baker Book House, 1974), 8:102.

PASTORAL PERSPECTIVE

A movie director would surely begin where Isaiah begins: by concentrating on the feet. Feet, running along a mountain path. Accustomed to such terrain they are practiced, swift, and deft. They are also dirty, dusty, calloused, perhaps even bleeding. What makes them beautiful is the message we hear when the focus widens to the runner's mouth: good tidings, peace, and the news that God reigns! The message itself, shouted aloud and borne aloft on the mountain air, arrives before the messenger.

The camera then moves to the sentries stationed upon the wall who have heard the message. The sentries are singing! And why wouldn't they be? After all we are told that they see the return of God "eye to eye." Moses spoke to God "face to face" (Exod. 33:11, Num. 12:8). Now the sentries see God eye to eye. The intimacy and immediacy of this act of divine self-revealing is disarming. The guards let down their guard and break into song.

The image of the ancient sentries, eye to eye with God and singing from their lookouts, forces the question: What does God look like? What does the return of God look like? What does God's reign feel like? For Christians that question is answered on Christmas morning. God looks like an infant. His name is Immanuel. Here is God's latest revealing: human and humble, a testimony to the yearning of our God to bridge the distance between us.

That bright truth does not end the conversation. Even with the gift of Jesus, we do not always experience God as reigning. Too often it feels as if God is nowhere to be found. On Christmas morning we are reminded that God rarely chooses to exercise God's sovereignty in the ways we expect or desire . . . or, for that matter, even notice. It is, therefore, a good morning for the church to wrestle with what it means to worship a God who appears in our midst as a child, poor and lowly and without weapons, crown, or wealth. In what ways do we honor our God's style of reigning? How do we imitate it, practice it, and teach it?

The camera proceeds to pan the crumbled walls and the vacant homes of those who were carried into exile. The lens rolls over Jerusalem's dilapidated structures and looted shops, as even these are invited to join the singing. It is a magical image, but one that evokes the symbiotic relationship between human community and the architecture of beloved and familiar places . . . places where babies were born, couples married, children raised, and grandparents buried. These are places that, brick by brick, had been built by the sweat of self, neighbors, and sons. In Isaiah's image, the city itself sings out a song of welcome to God and to Israel.

What does locale (home, meeting house, geography, city or town, village or countryside, school or cemetery) mean to your congregation? How do these participate in forming the human community that is at the heart of the divine invitation? On Christmas morning our homes and sanctuaries are festooned with greenery, candles, trees, lights, and other decorations so that they too may participate with us and share in the celebration of this day. The gift of this child through whom and in whom we see God eye to eye is cause for a party day, a feast day. One and all—sentient and inanimate—take up the festivities. The pastor may wish to contemplate how to capture and express in the liturgy and sermon the exultant joy of Isaiah's proclamation.

One possibility is to recall that Christmas Day is a day for singing, a day for carols. As the church will undergo a long fast from carols until this time next year, it is well to gorge on them now while they are plentiful. Martin Luther, who loved Christmas, claimed that "music is a fair and glorious gift of God." Music, he said, "makes people kinder, gentler, more staid and reasonable. The devil flees before the sound of music almost as much as before the Word of God."[2] Providing opportunity for the congregation to sing well and joyfully, to sing loudly, confidently, and with abandon, to break forth into singing with the ancient sentinels and the waste places of Jerusalem, will no doubt require some planning. It is not the natural proclivity of all congregations to sing with abandon, heads up and voices raised. The pastor who prepares carefully and enables the congregation to sing out will find that it has been well worth the effort.

Singing our carols as if we mean them is one way to express the profound implications of Isaiah's message: that the Lord has comforted his people. How can you help your congregation feel this, believe it, and live into it? Nietzsche is said to have complained that the trouble with Christians is that they don't look redeemed. Christmas Day is a day we had better look and act redeemed. The pastor will want to model this by looking and acting both redeemed and comforted in a way that is convincing to the congregation!

The passage began with a camera trained on the feet of a messenger. It moved to the watchmen, swept over Jerusalem, and rested for a moment on a people comforted. For the final scene the camera pulls back until the viewer can take in all the nations, indeed, all the ends of the earth. This is no parochial God who reigns over a tribal community. This is John of Patmos's God of gods, King of kings, and Lord of lords (Rev. 19:16). This is the one God to whom the whole earth belongs. Isaiah announces that it is this God and none other who has returned and whose reign is now inaugurated.

NANCY S. TAYLOR

2. From the foreword to the *Wittenberg Gesangbuch* (1524), Martin Luther's hymnbook.

EXEGETICAL PERSPECTIVE

A sense of anticipation runs throughout the prophetic poetry of Isaiah 40–55, a section of the book of Isaiah dating to the end of the Babylonian exile (587–538 BCE). Following the destruction of Jerusalem and its temple and the decades spent in Babylon, many exiled Judahites concluded that their God had abandoned them (Isa. 40:27; 49:14). Second Isaiah—the scholarly designation for the prophet(s) behind these chapters—insists that YHWH is about to move decisively, despite the recent appearance of inactivity, to bring the exiles home and restore Israel's glory. Nowhere is this sense of anticipation more immediate than in Isaiah 52:7–10, which declares that the nation's salvation is "in plain sight" (v. 8). This vividness of presence makes these verses especially apt readings for Christmas Day worship.

These verses form part of a larger poem about the future of Jerusalem, also referred to as Zion, in Isaiah 51:17–52:12, which in turn belongs to a series of alternating poems about the servant of YHWH and Jerusalem/Zion in Isaiah 49–54. The passage brings together a number of important themes and characteristic terminology from Isaiah 40–55, which indicates its important place within these chapters.

Verse 7 opens with an exclamation, "How beautiful!" The term "beautiful" (*n'h*) appears in Song of Solomon as an expression of physical attraction to one's lover, often referring to a particular body part like the cheeks or mouth (Song 1:5, 10; 2:14; 4:3; 6:4). The target of the description here is also a body part, but a surprisingly mundane one: the feet. Although hardly attractive in themselves, these feet prove beautiful because they belong to a "messenger" (*mebasser*) who has traveled over great distance and difficult terrain ("upon the mountains") with an important announcement. While the messenger's identity is unimportant for the meaning of the passage, commentators have variously identified the figure as a prophet or an angel, while Paul reinterprets the verse as a reference to early Christian missionaries to the Gentiles (Rom. 10:15).

In Isaiah 40:9, Jerusalem/Zion itself is called a "herald of good tidings" (*mebassret*), the feminine counterpart of the term translated "messenger" here in Isaiah 52:7, where Zion is clearly the recipient of the message. Successive phrases characterize the messenger as one "who announces peace," "brings good news," and "announces salvation." These vague but suggestive descriptions heighten suspense before the content of the message is revealed at the end of the verse: "Your God reigns."

The notion of God's kingship finds expression throughout the OT, with the specific declaration "God/YHWH reigns" occurring primarily in the

Psalms (Pss. 47:9; 93:1; 96:10; etc.). This confession gains new significance in the exilic context of Isaiah 51 as a counterclaim to Babylonian belief in the superiority of their supreme deity, Marduk. Note especially the statement "Marduk is king!" in the Babylonian creation myth (*Enuma Elish* 4.28).[3]

Verse 8 describes the reaction to this message. Sentinels were an important part of a city's defense, standing watch for threats from the vantage of the city's fortifications (2 Sam. 18:24–27; 2 Kgs. 9:17–20; Ezek. 33:2–6; etc.). Instead of the expected cry of warning, these sentinels respond to the messenger's appearance with enthusiastic song, more like a choir than a military unit. Their joy results from their recognition of "the return of the LORD to Zion." As vividly depicted in Ezekiel 10, many Judahites believed that YHWH had abandoned Jerusalem during the exile. The proclamation of God's return to the city follows from the earlier confession of divine kingship, since Jerusalem was viewed as the earthly locus of God's reign (Pss. 48:1–2; 87:1–3; 146:10; etc.). The phrase "in plain sight" literally means "eye to eye" (*'ayin be'ayin*), and this body language—along with references to the messenger's feet in verse 7 and God's arm in verse 10—imparts an air of physicality to the poem.

In verse 9a, the prophet commands the personified ruins of the city to join the sentinels in their jubilation, repeating the words "break forth . . . into singing" (*rnn*) and "together" (*yahdaw*) from verse 8. Similar calls to praise are common in biblical hymns (e.g., Ps. 100), as is the verb *rnn*, and the occurrence of these features here evokes the atmosphere of that genre. The imperative verbs directed toward Jerusalem continue a string of such verbs in the larger poem (Isa. 51:17; 52:1–2). Even as the text looks forward to Jerusalem's imminent restoration, the use of the term "ruins" acknowledges the devastated state of a city not yet rebuilt, and belies the reference to sentinels in the previous verse as a bold act of poetic imagination.

Having depicted YHWH's activity largely from the perspective of its observers in verses 7–9, Second Isaiah now describes it directly. Verse 9b provides the motivation for the preceding call to praise. The statement that YHWH "has comforted [*nhm*] his people" marks the fulfillment of Isaiah 40:1 ("Comfort, O comfort my people"), and the verb "redeem" (*g'l*) occurs frequently in Isaiah 40–55 (Isa. 41:14; 44:22–23; 48:20; etc.). Although these actions remain in the future, the verbs appear in the perfect tense in Hebrew, as indicated by their translation in the NRSV, reflecting the prophet's certainty that they will happen. The baring of God's "holy arm" in verse 10 is

---

3. See "Epic of Creation," trans. Benjamin R. Foster, in *The Context of Scripture*, ed. W. W. Hallo, 3 vols. (Boston: Brill, 2003), 1.111:390–402.

a display of divine power. This motif recalls the opening vision of Second Isaiah (Isa. 40:10) and anticipates the fourth Servant Song, which almost immediately follows this passage (Isa. 52:13–53:12). Alluding to the exodus, with which the motif of the divine arm is frequently associated in the OT (Exod. 6:6; Deut. 5:15; Ps. 136:12; etc.), the prophet had called upon "the arm of the LORD" to "awake" and "put on strength . . . as in days of old" in the previous chapter (Isa. 51:9).

That prayer has now been answered. This display of power takes place "before the eyes of all the nations" (v. 10), continuing the emphasis upon vision in these verses. Just as the other nations witnessed Jerusalem's humiliation in its defeat and exile, they will soon see its restoration and the return of its people. This unprecedented marvel will provide powerful evidence of God's rule over the entire world, which these verses both announce and call God's people to celebrate.

J. BLAKE COUEY

HOMILETICAL PERSPECTIVE

Hearing this text at Christmas may call to mind the hymn "Joy to the World": it is a rousing invitation to join together in full-voiced praise of God. In the oracle, the prophet imagines heralds proclaiming good news to the city of Zion and envisions the joyful response of the people, and of the city itself, to God's saving action.

Have you ever thought of your preaching as doxological—as an act of praise to God? Have you ever considered that your preaching leads into the doxology of the congregation—that it inspires the congregation to praise? This joyful text provides you with a perfect opportunity to explore these homiletical possibilities. The prophet imagines that sentinels are on the city walls singing for joy, and then tells Zion to break into song. The prophet's call echoes Psalm 98:4: "Make a joyful noise to the LORD, all the earth; break forth into joyous song and sing praises." It is as if the prophet is seeing the fulfillment of the psalmist's hope and proclaiming to the city, "It's happening! Start up the band!"

To reflect on the preaching possibilities of this call to praise, you could start by considering various ways in which people praise God. One way is through testimony, through stories of God's activity in their lives. What stories of God's reign and victory can be told from the life of your congregation and community? Perhaps you could share the stories of others as part of your sermon, or maybe they could share their testimony themselves. These testimonies point to the ongoing work of God, who bares "his holy arm before the eyes of all the nations" (v. 10). You could also draw on another mode of praise, which is in the text: singing. What songs of praise are familiar and loved in your congregation? Could the words of these songs be woven into the sermon, or could the congregation sing a song of praise as part of the sermon? Singing songs of praise is a way in which the community participates in the continuing joyful doxology of all creation.

The call for praise in the text takes on deeper meaning when we reflect on the place and the people from which the song will arise. In an act of profoundly faithful imagination, the prophet takes his exiles with him to the broken walls of Jerusalem. The prophet hears the sentinels on the walls, and says to the people in the city, "Break forth together into singing, you ruins of Jerusalem" (v. 9). The city that is crumbling under foreign occupation can now rejoice: God is returning, the city will be restored, and the community will be made whole. The prophet describes this future with certainty, as an accomplished fact, a fact that calls for songs of praise.

This is an opportunity for you to consider the social location of the congregation. Do ruins surround your congregation? What are they? What songs of praise can you all imagine arising from this place? It might seem incongruent for those who live in fear of violence and in grinding poverty, with broken homes and communities, to sing praise—but these are they to whom the prophet cries, "Sing!" The child who is born and the promise of God's coming kingdom are for all who live among ruins.

So far we have been imagining the congregation as those who live in the ruined city. You could also picture the congregation as the sentinels who call to the city. In the oracle, the prophet sees a messenger running across the mountains bringing good news. Sentinels are posted along the city walls, listening to hear the messengers announce the king's arrival, and watching to glimpse the returning of the king. In the text, the sentinels hear the messenger and "lift up their voices, together they sing for joy" (v. 8). Their singing is a proclamation of good news to the city, calling forth songs of praise.

Imagine the members of your congregation as sentinels, standing watch in the community, looking and listening for signs of God's reign breaking into the world. Where do you see God working in your community and in the world? Are there testimonies of God's activity that you could incorporate into the sermon? How can the sermon inspire the congregation to praise God? For whom is your congregation a sentinel, and for whom might the congregation's praise be good news? This text can help form the congregation as witnesses to the world, sentinels who sing of the God they have seen and heard in Jesus Christ.

As you conclude your reflections on the text and begin to move toward the sermon, you will need to consider what form the sermon will take, and what kind of language you will use. Since the text is poetry, one possibility is to follow the text by crafting a poetic sermon that does what the text does. You could invite the congregation to sing a song of praise to God, as those who dwell in the city to which God is returning, and to sing so that others will sing as well.

In his moving history *There Is a River: The Black Struggle for Freedom in America*, Vincent Harding tells a story that may prompt you to reflect further on the scene of rejoicing in the text. He recounts the celebration of freed slaves in Richmond, Virginia, at the sight of black and white Union troops after the surrender of the city near the end of the American Civil War. As songs and shouts echoed back and forth between marching troops and cascading crowds, the multitude descended upon Richmond's infamous slave market. There, on the ruins of oppression, they proclaimed freedom to all people in a scene that Harding imagines could have evoked a turning point in history.[4]

Can you envision this scene: songs and shouts echoing in the war-torn city, the jubilant proclamation of those who are free? Allow it to open your imagination as a sign and foretaste of the celebration envisioned by the prophet: God is returning to God's holy city, and all will be freed to worship and praise God forevermore.

PATRICK W. T. JOHNSON

John 1:1–14

THEOLOGICAL PERSPECTIVE

"But, as a matter of fact, another part of my trade, too, made me sure you weren't a priest."

"What?" asked the thief, almost gaping.

"You attacked reason," said Father Brown. "It's bad theology."[5]

The thief disguised as a priest had been trying to convince Father Brown—G. K. Chesterton's priest-detective—of his priestly credentials by disparaging reason. Evidently he thought it was the religious thing to do: to gaze reverently at the heavens and claim not merely that the mysteries of the universe exceeded our understanding but that they made reason itself

---

4. Vincent Harding, *There Is a River: The Black Struggle for Freedom in America* (New York: Harcourt Brace Jovanovich, 1981), 275.
5. G. K. Chesterton, "The Blue Cross," in *The Innocence of Father Brown* (New York: Penguin Books, 1975), 29.

"utterly unreasonable." Father Brown knew better. "Reason and justice," he affirmed, "grip the remotest and the loneliest star."[6]

Our text, constituting most of the prologue to the Fourth Gospel, is one of several sources in Christian Scripture to which he might have appealed in support of that affirmation. (Others frequently cited in conjunction with this text are Ps. 33:6; Prov. 8; Col. 1:16–17; and Heb. 1:2.) All creation is imbued with the Logos, the Word and Wisdom of God. All creation bears witness to the primordial, sense-making Word through which it has come to be and in which it finds its coherence. Thanks to this formative and informing Wisdom, creation is not only intelligible but intelligent, sense-seeking, and sense-honoring. Creaturely reality is marked by a lively participation—in ways appropriate to various, finite, contingent, sojourning creatures—in the Truth that is with God, and that is God.

All this is affirmed by Christian traditions generally, but the affirmation is accompanied by a sober acknowledgment that, however it may be with the remotest star, we human creatures, at least, have seriously strayed from our calling to honor reason and justice. Having long ago exchanged the truth for a lie (Rom. 1:25), we seem intent on leaving reason and justice behind, while busily making up our own substitutes and giving those substitutes the name of the real thing. What often passes for reason with us is a truncated form of this capacity, sometimes called "instrumental rationality": the ability to manipulate and control things (and persons) as objects, for our own purposes. What often passes for justice is the arrangement of laws and legal systems by the powerful to serve the interests of the powerful. This is "the wisdom of this world" that is indeed "foolishness with God" (1 Cor. 3:19). It should not be confused with the genuine article.

When discussing human beings' rational capacity, our theological forebears sometimes made a sober and useful distinction between *created* reason and *fallen* reason. Created reason—the human mind as it was meant to be, and as it was thought by these writers to have been exercised by Adam and Eve in the original human "state of integrity" in the garden of Eden—participated rightly in the Logos that informs reality. What we know and experience now in our post-Edenic state is fallen reason, reason that is corrupt and corrupting, and a twin to injustice. (Recall how close is the tie between injustice and the willing misrepresentation of reality: "Ah, you who call evil good and good evil, who put darkness for light and light for darkness, who put bitter for sweet and sweet for bitter!" [Isa. 5:20].) This latter form of reason (if it can be called that) deserves all the censure it has received at

6. Ibid., 24.

the hands of Paul and subsequent generations of Christian thinkers, so long as it is clear that the target of censure is this distortion and corruption of a created good, and not reason as such.

Unfortunately, that has not always been made clear. Christians have at times indulged in assaults on reason itself, contrasting it to faith. The sometimes popular tendency to associate Christianity with anti-intellectualism, opposition to scientific knowledge, and authoritarian thought control gains support from such undiscriminating talk. That is not the message of the gospel. Christ, the one Paul calls "the wisdom of God" (1 Cor. 1:24) and whom our Johannine author knows as Word and Light, came not to destroy reason but to restore us to it: to bring us to our senses.

Our forebears spoke not only of "created" and "fallen" reason but also of *regenerate* reason, reason reborn. One aspect of the "second birth" that Christ brings to the sons and daughters of earth is a rebirth of understanding: the onset of a recovery of the human capacity to honor the truth. "The Word became flesh and lived among us" (v. 14). The Wisdom of God seeks friendship with us, in tangible, vulnerable, human form. (Making a connection with 2 Cor. 8:9, Gustavo Gutiérrez and others have suggested that the most apt contemporary equivalent to "the Word became flesh" may be "the Word became poor."[7]) This gracious disclosure of reality not only unmasks our own current pitiful practices of "reason" and "justice," but sets us on a different path, toward the renewing of our minds (Rom. 12:2).

We are embarked on a journey of transformation. We are not there yet. There is much to unlearn, as well as much to learn, as we are led into the truth under the guidance of the Spirit of truth of whose coming Jesus spoke (John 16:13). One of the constant themes of the Fourth Gospel is the importance of the community of faith, both as a context for growth in understanding and as a witness to the power of Truth incarnate. The work of Christ and the work of the Spirit are inseparable in this process through which, together, we are renewed through the one whose coming to dwell among us we celebrate this day.

CHARLES M. WOOD

PASTORAL PERSPECTIVE

For many Protestant Christians, the opportunity to worship on Christmas Day is limited to those few years when Christmas falls on a Sunday. The wisdom of ceding a holy day to (rampant) consumerism and (over) eating

---

7. Gustavo Gutiérrez, "God's Revelation and Proclamation in History," in *The Power of the Poor in History*, trans. Robert R. Barr (Maryknoll, NY: Orbis Books, 1983), 12–13.

aside, it is certainly the case that the common practice of not worshiping on Christmas Day leads to a compressed, if not truncated, Christmas celebration. In Roman Catholic and other more traditional liturgical churches, the Christmas experience *begins* rather than *concludes* on Christmas Eve.

Reclaiming Christmas Day also entails recasting Christmas Eve. In the expanded two-day celebration, Christmas Eve is focused on expectation and anticipation at its peak. Mary and Joseph arrive at the place of nativity and, like any expectant father and mother, find themselves embroiled in the hustle and bustle that immediately precedes birth. As nurses or midwives attend, the anticipation of mother and father mounts until . . . finally . . . that moment of delivery! The night both peaks and concludes with "Joy to the World." Christmas Day, on the other hand, is for settling in. As with a typical birth experience, the crowds are mostly dispersed. Mother and father have time to spend alone with the newborn child. Exhausted and overwhelmed by the previous night's events, words are used sparely. Punctuated perhaps by naps, snacks, and short visits, it is a day for the quiet realization that life will never again be the same. The question of the moment is, "What Child Is This?"[8]

The prologue to the Gospel of John is legendary for the exegetical, theological, and homiletical challenges it presents. Few other passages of the Bible have been subjected to as much prolonged and varied scrutiny as this one. Fortunately, the pastoral question for Christmas Day is narrower and, though potentially aided by the vast history of interpretation, does not require it: How does this passage help us to "settle in" to life with the newborn savior who will change our lives forever?

When compared to the very concrete narrative of the Gospel text suggested for Christmas Eve (Luke 2:1–20), the poetic language of John 1:1–14 seems almost to float untethered from daily life. Pregnant women, kicking babies, a decreeing emperor, weary travelers, a swaddled baby, visiting shepherds—John's version offers no such enticing details and characterizations as it begins the gospel story. Instead we have the language of mystery: "In the beginning was the Word, and the Word was with God, and the Word was God." Our desire to be entertained is thwarted. But our need to be grounded is met, paradoxically, in this vision of a savior who refuses to be pinned down to overly precise human expectations.

In avoiding the temptation to wish poetry away, we are rewarded with a text that can be our quiet companion on this day of watching and listening

8. I am indebted to my colleague and friend the Rev. Don Bailey-François for his reflections on the rhythm of these days.

for the signs of life's new meaning. The prologue is what literary critic Frank Kermode aptly called a "threshold poem," concerned with "how that which *was* crossed over into *becoming*."[9] Its nuanced words, while frustrating to the prosaic mind, offer a fountain of resources for probing the liminality of Christmas Day. Before the birth we were not alone. We knew God and worshiped God. But now our knowing is different, and our worship can never again be the same. We are crossing a threshold.

Over against Luke's "cast of thousands," John's prologue contains only three "characters" (if we can even properly call them that). Two of them, God and the Word, overlap in a complex and (humanly) difficult way. The third, John the Baptist, seems oddly and abruptly inserted into the poem's flow. Verses 6–9 remind us that Jesus has a prehistory. Like every child who is born, he is part of a family legacy. John's presence in the poem ties Jesus to ancient Israel and to the prophetic tradition. This savior of the world is also a human being with a particular identity that may embarrass us in some circles. He isn't timeless, or universal, or generically spiritual. He was born at a specific time, to a specific people, who practiced a specific religion. He is also tied to a tradition that places fidelity to God's truth above the niceties of diplomacy. He is likely to cause some trouble.

The verses before and after John's appearance in the poem literally foreshadow the trouble that is to come. This birth brings light to the world, but that light will be made more visible by the surrounding darkness. Light is defined by the shadows that surround it. Every parent knows that a newborn infant will both face, and cause, difficulties as he or she grows up. The poem's realism, while not detailed in prediction, is absolute in conviction. Darkness exists. It is real and terrifying. But the light of life will persist and prevail. One ancient commentator captures the drama superbly: the life that is light "is chased by the darkness, but is not overtaken by it."[10]

So, while Christmas Day is a day replete with worry and foreboding, it is ultimately a day of hope. Verse 14 makes the promise explicit. The Word has encamped among us, we have seen glory, a glory full of grace and truth. We receive that promise only in faith. John refuses to pin down our hopes to anything more specific than the One who was, and is becoming, the Word. Like parents of a newborn, we are startled that we would be released back

9. "John," in *The Literary Guide to the Bible*, ed. Robert Alter and Frank Kermode (Cambridge, MA: Harvard University Press, 1987), 445.
10. Gregory of Nazianzus, *Oration 39*, in *The Nicene and Post-Nicene Fathers, Second Series*, vol. 7, ed. Philip Schaff and Henry Wace (Peabody, MA: Hendrickson Publishers, 1994), 685.

into the world with such vagaries. Should we not have to pass a test? Could a nurse come to live with us and show us what to do? Is there a list of rules to keep us all safe? No, there is just the Child—his life and presence—and the promise of "grace upon grace" (John 1:17) that unfolds in the chapters ahead.

MICHAEL S. BENNETT

EXEGETICAL PERSPECTIVE

In contrast to Matthew and Luke, Mark and John write nothing about Jesus' birth, but instead begin the story about Jesus with John the Baptist. John the evangelist, however, prefaces the earthly story with a heavenly story: "In the beginning was the Word, and the Word was with God, and the Word was God. . . . All things came into being through [the Word; NRSV "him"]" (vv. 1, 3a).

The Greek pronoun translated "him" in verse 3 is ambiguous; it can also mean "it." "Word" is an abstract noun; it does not designate a heavenly person. These verses echo Genesis 1:1, "In the beginning God created . . ." John is not saying that the Word created, but that God created through God's Word. In Genesis 1, God creates by *speaking*: "God *said*, 'Let there be light,' and there was light" (Gen. 1:3). The Word is not a heavenly being distinct from God but a function of God in creation. There is a parallel in Isaiah 55:11: "so shall my word be that goes out from my mouth; it shall not return to me empty, but it shall accomplish that which I purpose."

In Proverbs, Wisdom is assigned a role in God's creation: "The LORD by wisdom founded the earth" (Prov. 3:19; see also Wis. 7:22, "wisdom, the fashioner of all things"). The personification of God's Wisdom is carried much further in Sirach 24. Since the word for "wisdom" in Hebrew and in Greek is feminine, Wisdom is personified as a female person: "Wisdom praises herself, and tells of her glory" (v. 1); yet Sirach shrinks from presenting Wisdom as a goddess: "I came forth from the mouth of the Most High" (v. 3). John was perhaps influenced by this wisdom tradition, which attributed a role in creation to Wisdom, but in anticipation of verse 14, he preferred to use "Word," because in Greek this word is masculine.

The NRSV footnote offers an alternate translation of verse 9: "He was the true light that enlightens everyone coming into the world." This seems preferable to the standard translation, "The true light . . . was coming into the world," which suggests that the incarnation was an extended process. The illumination of everyone may then refer not to religious enlightenment but to the philosophical idea that all human beings possess reason as a divine gift. It is thus possible to see verses 9 and 10 as speaking about the preincarnational activity of God's Word. Verses 11–13, however, are postincarnational; they look back to the incarnation that has already occurred.

"He came to what was his own," or "to his own home," refers to the historical location of the incarnation in Jewish Palestine; "his own people" emphasizes the specific human context of the incarnation: Israel. Here the refusal of most Jews to accept Jesus is presented as a fact without any negative comment; later in the Gospel the mutual hostility of "Jews" and Christians becomes a major theme (see esp. chap. 8). Verse 12 implies that those who did not accept Jesus had no right to consider themselves children of God, despite the fact that they called God "Father" (Isa. 63:16; 64:8; see John 8:41–42).

The time implied by verses 12–13 is not clear: "all who received him" could refer to those who believed in Jesus prior to the crucifixion, or it could include all those who came to faith subsequently (John 20:29). The reference in verse 13 to being born of God anticipates 3:7, "You must be born from above."

The climax of the passage, of the whole Gospel—one might even dare to say of the whole New Testament—comes in verse 14: "And the Word became flesh and lived among us." It is the chief foundation stone of the doctrine of the Trinity.

Christian interpreters have become so comfortable with this text that it no longer shocks us. It does, however, shock Jews and Muslims, because it seems sacrilegiously to blur the distinction between God and human beings. It shocks Unitarians, who see it as a fatal breach of monotheism. It can even be a source of discomfort to Christians as they ponder the question, Was Jesus a real human being or not? In what ways was he divine, in what ways was he human?

In the second century, Marcion promoted a revised version of Christianity. He taught that Jesus, a heavenly messenger of the highest god, arrived in Galilee having the appearance of a fully grown man. He taught that humans could escape the material world created by the evil god of the Jews and rise to the realm of pure spirit. His crucifixion and resurrection were pure charades. Some lines in John's Gospel may have encouraged Marcion, such as 6:38, "For I have come down from heaven." However, the Fourth Gospel, like the other three, is focused on Jesus' death as the central event in God's redemptive history. The crucifixion is no charade; the real death of a real man is involved.

John 1:14 does not teach us that Jesus was part God and part human. It is essential that we recognize that the divinity of Jesus, however we understand it, did not compromise his humanity. He did not know everything; he could not do everything. Jesus related to God the way we do: through prayer. In chapter 17 John presents Jesus as praying fervently to God on behalf of his followers. He pleads, "As you, Father, are in me and I am in you, may they also be in us" (v. 21). This verse offers another way of looking at the incarnation. It reminds us of Paul's statement, "In Christ God was reconciling" (2 Cor. 5:19).

It is best to take John's daring incarnational language dynamically rather than statically; that is, he did not intend to instruct his readers about "the two natures of Christ," still less, about the Son "being of one substance with the Father," as the Nicene Creed avers. He was concerned rather with what God accomplished through the unique relationship of Father and Son. John was saying that Jesus of Nazareth was yoked to God as no other human being ever was. Jesus' dying was a very human dying, but God and Jesus were one in his dying.

DOUGLAS R. A. HARE

HOMILETICAL PERSPECTIVE

The Gospel reading from John for Christmas Day, the passage often referred to as the prologue, is more poem than narrative. And poetic language is exactly what is called for, because John is doing something different from the writers of the Synoptics. Mark begins his Gospel with an account of John the Baptizer, whose baptism of Jesus is the occasion at which Jesus is identified as God's beloved child. Matthew's Gospel begins with the details of Jesus' genealogy and Joseph's doubt, and Luke's account begins with vivid descriptions of angelic appearances, first to Mary and then to the shepherds. Both Matthew and Luke make it clear that Jesus is known as the Son of God, even at his birth. In the Fourth Gospel, however, divine identity is clear from the inauguration of time. Long before taking on human flesh, Jesus, the Word, was with God "in the beginning"—even more, Jesus *was* God.[11] So perhaps only poetry will do to describe John's Jesus.

Incarnation and Redemption. As incomprehensible as it seems, the cosmic eternal Christ, the preexisting Logos, is also a flesh-and-blood person, who was born to a particular woman in a particular town at a particular time, and died a painful physical death. This incomprehensible mystery is, of course, what we mean when we talk about the central theme of Christmas,

11. See Alan Culpepper, *The Gospel and Letters of John* (Nashville: Abingdon Press, 1998), 110–11, for a fuller explication of the differences between the opening chapters of each Gospel.

the incarnation. Sylvia Dunstan is one modern-day poet who has tried to get at the inscrutability of it all, in her poem "Christus Paradox."

She writes of the apparent polarities that Christ himself embodies: lamb and shepherd, prince and slave, one who brings peace and one who brings the sword. Then she turns the paradox toward praise:

> Worthy your defeat and vict'ry.
> Worthy still your peace and strife.
> You, the everlasting instant;
> You, who are our death and life.[12]

The incarnation—that is, the whole life, death, and resurrection of Jesus— is at the very heart of the paschal mystery. This means, then, that we cannot celebrate Christmas without having Easter in view. One who preaches on Christmas cannot proclaim the birth of the baby Jesus without also proclaiming the purpose of that birth. For the wonder of the incarnation is that when Word becomes flesh, human history is irrevocably changed; the relationship between God and humanity is forever altered. Athanasius (fourth cent. CE), bishop of Alexandria and perhaps the church's greatest teacher on the incarnation, asserted that Jesus "became human that we might become God. He manifested Himself by means of a body in order that we might perceive the Mind of the unseen Father . . . [and] endured shame from men that we might inherit immortality."[13]

Incarnation and Revelation. It is not only that the Jesus who lived and died for us achieved our atonement through his suffering and sacrifice, overcoming our alienation to God and drawing us into God's own eternal life. That would be enough—but there is still more! In his living, dying, and rising, Christ reveals to us the God we could not otherwise know. Through the story of how Jesus came to be born, the narratives of his life and ministry, the account of his suffering and death, and the proclamation of his rising— not just as an ethereal spirit being but as a body who eats breakfast with his friends on the beach after overcoming death—through it all, the words and deeds of the incarnate Word, we somehow know more of who our God is. Of course we will never know it all, for what God has done for us in Christ reaches far beyond our most profound imaginings. As Athanasius put it,

---

12. Sylvia Dunstan, "Christus Paradox," in *In Search of Hope and Grace* (Chicago: GIA Publications, 1991).
13. Athanasius, *De incarnatione Verbi Dei* (New York: St. Vladimir's Seminary Press, 1975), §54.

"to try to number [all that Christ has done] is like gazing at the open sea and trying to count the waves." We cannot begin to take in all that Christ has accomplished, he says, "for the things that transcend one's thought are always more than those one thinks that one has grasped." All there is to do is gaze in awe at the amazing mystery and gift of Christmas and to sing our praise.

Incarnational Faith. All of this means that celebrating the birthday of Jesus goes much deeper than "keeping the Christ in Christmas." Preaching the doctrine of the incarnation does not mean explaining some dry theory or reciting some old, long-ago history. Nor does it mean caving in to the sentimentality of the season to which it is all too easy to succumb. Preachers must proclaim nothing less than Jesus Christ the living Word, the one who brought the cosmos into being, the one who will bring creation to completion, and the one who lives today—"who was and is and is to be, and still the same." We encounter him in the reading and preaching of the Word; he invites us to the Table and meets us there; he is present in his body, the church. This is why we live an incarnational faith—why we seek Jesus not only in the words we say but in the sacramental life we share. If we are paying attention, we recognize too that God is in the ordinary moments of our life—in the making of lunches and the folding of laundry, in daily kisses good-bye, in the moment when we look into the eyes of one whom the world considers unlovely at best and unworthy of notice at worst. It is why we aim to live the Christian life by not only talking about it or thinking about it, but by doing it—why our prayers are not only those of the heart, but those of the hands and the feet.

KIMBERLY BRACKEN LONG

❧ MIDWEEK SERVICES ☙

Introduction

The following devotional services, designed for use during a brief mid-week gathering, contain liturgies for opening and closing, two Scriptures, a homily, and prayers of confession and intercession. Depending on how much time you have, you may also want to include a hymn or song.

These services are ideal for use in an established morning prayer or lunchtime worship service or an evening Bible study. You may also want to use them for a short-term worship gathering that could be offered for the season of Advent. These services are a complement to Sunday morning worship, whether they are scheduled to precede or follow the four Sundays of Advent, allowing for flexibility depending on the fall of Christmas Day on the calendar.

The Gospel texts chosen for these services form a brief study of John the Baptist, which, paired with passages from the prophet Isaiah, explore the vocation of "preparing the way" for the Messiah.

Midweek Service: Week One

Isaiah 57:14–19

¹⁴It shall be said,
"Build up, build up, prepare the way,
remove every obstruction from my people's way."
¹⁵For thus says the high and lofty one
who inhabits eternity, whose name is Holy:
I dwell in the high and holy place,
and also with those who are contrite and humble in spirit,
to revive the spirit of the humble,
and to revive the heart of the contrite.
¹⁶For I will not continually accuse,
nor will I always be angry;
for then the spirits would grow faint before me,
even the souls that I have made.
¹⁷Because of their wicked covetousness I was angry;
I struck them, I hid and was angry;
but they kept turning back to their own ways.
¹⁸I have seen their ways, but I will heal them;
I will lead them and repay them with comfort,
creating for their mourners the fruit of the lips.
¹⁹Peace, peace, to the far and the near, says the Lord;
and I will heal them.

Luke 1:5–25 (optional, vv. 57–80)

⁵In the days of King Herod of Judea, there was a priest named Zechariah, who belonged to the priestly order of Abijah. His wife was a descendant of Aaron, and her name was Elizabeth. ⁶Both of them were righteous before God, living blamelessly according to all the commandments and regulations of the Lord. ⁷But they had no children, because Elizabeth was barren, and both were getting on in years.

⁸Once when he was serving as priest before God and his section was on duty, ⁹he was chosen by lot, according to the custom of the priesthood,

to enter the sanctuary of the Lord and offer incense. [10]Now at the time of the incense offering, the whole assembly of the people was praying outside. [11]Then there appeared to him an angel of the Lord, standing at the right side of the altar of incense. [12]When Zechariah saw him, he was terrified; and fear overwhelmed him. [13]But the angel said to him, "Do not be afraid, Zechariah, for your prayer has been heard. Your wife Elizabeth will bear you a son, and you will name him John. [14]You will have joy and gladness, and many will rejoice at his birth, [15]for he will be great in the sight of the Lord. He must never drink wine or strong drink; even before his birth he will be filled with the Holy Spirit. [16]He will turn many of the people of Israel to the Lord their God. [17]With the spirit and power of Elijah he will go before him, to turn the hearts of parents to their children, and the disobedient to the wisdom of the righteous, to make ready a people prepared for the Lord." [18]Zechariah said to the angel, "How will I know that this is so? For I am an old man, and my wife is getting on in years." [19]The angel replied, "I am Gabriel. I stand in the presence of God, and I have been sent to speak to you and to bring you this good news. [20]But now, because you did not believe my words, which will be fulfilled in their time, you will become mute, unable to speak, until the day these things occur."

[21]Meanwhile the people were waiting for Zechariah, and wondered at his delay in the sanctuary. [22]When he did come out, he could not speak to them, and they realized that he had seen a vision in the sanctuary. He kept motioning to them and remained unable to speak. [23]When his time of service was ended, he went to his home.

[24]After those days his wife Elizabeth conceived, and for five months she remained in seclusion. She said, [25]"This is what the Lord has done for me when he looked favorably on me and took away the disgrace I have endured among my people."

ORDER OF WORSHIP

OPENING WORDS / CALL TO WORSHIP

Build up, build up, prepare the way,   *Isa. 57:14–15*
remove every obstruction from my people's way.
The Holy One calls and we will answer;
revive our spirits, Lord, and bring peace to
    our longing souls.

CALL TO CONFESSION

The Lord is with those who are contrite   *Isa. 57:15*
and humble in spirit.
Let us trust in God's mercy as we confess our sins.

PRAYER OF CONFESSION

Faithful God, you have sent us prophets
and we have not listened.
We have turned away from you and
from one another,   *Luke 1:16–17*
tending to our own ways, rather than
making way for your reign.
We have chosen silence over proclamation.   *Luke 1:19–20*
Forgive us, we pray, and renew your covenant
within us,
for the sake of Jesus Christ, our Lord. Amen.

DECLARATION OF FORGIVENESS

Friends, I am confident of this:
if we repent, God is sure to forgive us.
The Lord has looked favorably on his people
and redeemed them.   *Luke 1:68*
Grateful for the promise of joy and of peace,
let us share that peace with one another.

PRAYER OF THE DAY

Covenant God, you send us messengers to
cleanse and refine us for your coming.
Help us endure the mirror of the prophets' message,
that we may see you when you suddenly
appear among us;
through Jesus Christ. **Amen.**

SCRIPTURE READINGS

HOMILY

Humility is rare among leaders these days. You hardly ever hear a CEO say, "Well, our success was not all because of me. There was someone who came before me who really prepared the way." No politician would ever stop to thank the person she replaced from her rival party. Leaders portray themselves as masters of the turnaround, as if nothing good happened until they got there to turn around the general incompetence of the organization. Often such leaders are called "saviors."

So it is interesting that when it comes to Jesus, the real savior, modesty makes an appearance. The Bible makes it clear that before he arrived on the scene, even Jesus had some help with the prep work.

All four Gospels show how John the Baptist prepared the way, echoing the words of the prophets, who said, "See, I am sending my messenger ahead of you, who will prepare your way; the voice of one crying out in the wilderness: 'Prepare the way of the Lord, make his paths straight.'"[1] John indeed goes out into the wilderness, baptizing people and proclaiming the advent of God's kingdom.

In Luke's Gospel, however, John is preparing the way for Jesus even in utero. Today's Gospel reading is part of Luke's extended and interlaced birth narratives of John the Baptist and Jesus (1:5–2:52), which precede the respective public appearance of both men, in the same order. Biblical birth narratives—for example, of Jacob, Moses, Samson, and Samuel—tend to accompany concrete instances of historical salvation, hence the pertinence to Luke's main theme: the arrival of the messianic savior. Jesus and John the Baptist, whose birth is unmentioned in the other Gospels, are intimately related—Luke makes them relatives—because both are the working of "the Lord . . . God, my savior" and the fulfillment of what "God spoke to our ancestors."

Zechariah is visited by the angel Gabriel to receive news of John's conception several months before Mary receives a similar visit to learn that she too will become pregnant. Like Gabriel's proclamation to Mary that her child will be called "Son of the Most High," Zechariah too receives a promise that the child his wife Elizabeth bears will be "great in the sight of the Lord . . . filled with the Holy Spirit," and not only that, but that he will have "the spirit and power of Elijah."

The portrayal of John as an Elijah presence heightens awareness of the apocalyptic overtones of the presentation, recalling not only the saving activity of God in the past, but also the understanding that with Elijah all prophecy ceased—until the coming of the Messiah. Though not mentioned in Luke, Matthew's and Mark's description of the adult John's clothing and

---

1. Though Mark 1:2a claims to be quoting Isaiah, Mark 1:2b actually cites Malachi 3:1. Mark 1:3 does, in fact, quote Isaiah 40:3.

eating habits quickly brings the image of Elijah (2 Kgs. 1:8) to the minds of readers/hearers, then and now. The likening of John to Elijah is more than just camel hair deep, however, resting at the core of John's mission as prophet of the Most High.

In foreshadowing John's prophetic role, Luke refers to the last verses of Malachi, in which God promises to send Elijah to "turn the hearts of parents to their children and the hearts of children to their parents." Likewise, John will turn parents and children to one another, and also "turn many of the people of Israel to the Lord their God."

Ironically, Zechariah's heart seems turned at first from both God and his child, as he is chastised like Sarah so many generations before for expressing disbelief that he and Elizabeth might have a child at their age. He is made mute for the duration of Elizabeth's pregnancy, proclaiming neither glory to God nor belief in his son's unique calling.

By contrast, Elizabeth bears witness to what the Lord has done for her, and when her cousin Mary arrives from Galilee with her own news, the women experience one of the most famous "recognition scenes" of all time, extraordinary because the recognition is utterly intrauterine! The spiritual commotion of fetal John—his own first prophecy—turns Elizabeth into a prophet: she is "filled with the Holy Spirit" and utters a prophetic blessing: Mary is "blessed . . . among women" even as the "fruit of [her] womb" is "blessed." To the usual blessing of progeny is added the supreme blessing of becoming "the mother of my Lord," the bearer of the "beloved son" of God. Elizabeth makes the important connection between Mary's blessing and Mary's believing what God spoke to her through the angel; an implicit contrast is with Zechariah's doubtful response.

John shows us what it means to prepare the way for the Messiah, calling attention to and celebrating Jesus at every opportunity, and prompting others to see and celebrate Jesus as well. Soon after his birth, John's influence expands to include his father and their neighbors as Zechariah's silence is broken at John's circumcision and naming ceremony.

Among the first words he utters after at least nine months of silence, Zechariah's song, like Advent, celebrates the new era to be brought by the incarnation—a fulfillment of God's promise of deliverance—and identifies John as one who makes way for the work of the incarnation by delivering knowledge about salvation and forgiveness.

From the beginning, John embraces his role as the predecessor, the pre-parer, the prophet pointing the way to Jesus, never trying to claim credit or acclaim for himself. There were probably people in the captivated crowds around grown-up John the Baptizer who told him he was the greatest, the savior of the world. But instead, John looked out to the future with a humble heart and imagined the one who would really get the job done.

Charismatic godly figures come and go, from Elijah to Isaiah to John. In fact, preparers of the way still appear today. We may be preparers ourselves. But there is only one savior of the world, and in Advent, we wait for him, turning our hearts to God and one another as we all turn our eyes to the one who is to come.

PRAYERS OF INTERCESSION
[A brief time of silence may be kept after each intercession.]
Loving God, through the gift of prayer
you teach us to hold one another in our hearts.

Hear now our prayers:

for the leaders and people of every nation:
for the church and all who serve the Lord:
for those who suffer in sorrow and affliction:
for refugees and travelers far from home:
for all who are in prison or facing trial:
for those who sit in darkness, or in the shadow of death: *Luke 1:79*

Gracious God, this is our prayer:
that your love will overflow more and more
in our lives, in your church, and in all the world,
until all may know the compassion of Christ Jesus,
our Savior and Lord, in whose name we pray. **Amen.**

DISMISSAL
The Lord who dwells in the high and holy place   *Isa. 57:15*
also walks with us to revive our hearts
and guide our feet in the path of peace.   *Luke 1:79*

Midweek Service: Week Two

Isaiah 40:1–11

¹Comfort, O comfort my people,
    says your God.
²Speak tenderly to Jerusalem,
    and cry to her
that she has served her term,
    that her penalty is paid,
that she has received from the Lord's hand
    double for all her sins.

³A voice cries out:
  "In the wilderness prepare the way of the Lord,
    make straight in the desert a highway for our God.
⁴Every valley shall be lifted up,
    and every mountain and hill be made low;
the uneven ground shall become level,
    and the rough places a plain.
⁵Then the glory of the Lord shall be revealed,
    and all people shall see it together,
    for the mouth of the Lord has spoken."

⁶A voice says, "Cry out!"
    And I said, "What shall I cry?"
 All people are grass,
    their constancy is like the flower of the field.
⁷The grass withers, the flower fades,
    when the breath of the Lord blows upon it;
    surely the people are grass.
⁸The grass withers, the flower fades;
    but the word of our God will stand forever.
⁹Get you up to a high mountain,
    O Zion, herald of good tidings;
lift up your voice with strength,
 O Jerusalem, herald of good tidings,

lift it up, do not fear;
say to the cities of Judah,
"Here is your God!"
^{10}See, the Lord GOD comes with might,
and his arm rules for him;
his reward is with him,
and his recompense before him.
^{11}He will feed his flock like a shepherd;
he will gather the lambs in his arms,
and carry them in his bosom,
and gently lead the mother sheep.

Mark 1:1–8

^{1}The beginning of the good news of Jesus Christ, the Son of God.
^{2}As it is written in the prophet Isaiah,
"See, I am sending my messenger ahead of you,
who will prepare your way;
^{3}the voice of one crying out in the wilderness:
'Prepare the way of the Lord,
make his paths straight,'"
^{4}John the baptizer appeared in the wilderness, proclaiming a baptism of repentance for the forgiveness of sins. ^{5}And people from the whole Judean countryside and all the people of Jerusalem were going out to him, and were baptized by him in the river Jordan, confessing their sins. ^{6}Now John was clothed with camel's hair, with a leather belt around his waist, and he ate locusts and wild honey. ^{7}He proclaimed, "The one who is more powerful than I is coming after me; I am not worthy to stoop down and untie the thong of his sandals. ^{8}I have baptized you with water; but he will baptize you with the Holy Spirit."

ORDER OF WORSHIP

OPENING WORDS / CALL TO WORSHIP
Proclaim the good news: *Mark 1:4*
Forgiveness is coming!
Shout to the Lord:
Salvation is here!

CALL TO CONFESSION

Let us confess our sins before God   *Mark 1:4–5*
who responds to repentance with forgiveness.

PRAYER OF CONFESSION

Like the flowers of the field, our faithfulness wavers,   *Isa. 40:6–7*
blowing with every breeze and withering in the heat.
We are inconstant, imperfect.
We proclaim compassion,   *Isa. 40:3–4*
but leave those in the valley low, crying out for bread.
We proclaim justice,
but leave the lofty high above the lowly.
We proclaim the Lord with our lips,
but do not prepare the way with our lives.
Forgive our hypocrisy, and level our hearts, Lord,
that we may serve you. Amen.

DECLARATION OF FORGIVENESS

Arise, for your penalty is paid.   *Isa. 40:11*
The Lord gives comfort to the contrite in heart;
the Shepherd gathers his lambs in a warm embrace.

PRAYER OF THE DAY

Gracious Lord, we praise your holy name.
Your mighty acts are matched only by your compassion,
which softens our hard hearts and turns them toward your people.
Give us strong voices and loving hands
to proclaim your good tidings through all the earth,
in the name of your son, our Lord, Jesus Christ. **Amen.**

SCRIPTURE READINGS

HOMILY

Imagine you live in Galilee around 70 CE. There is a war on. Some radical Jews have revolted against Rome, and Jerusalem is under siege. Reports are that conditions in the city are bad. People are divided. Some see God raising up leaders to push the infidels from the Holy Land. Others urge submission to Rome as the path to peace and security. Everyone is anxious, caught between resentment of heavy-handed soldiers and fear of extremist guerrillas. Furthermore, Emperor Nero died last year, and there is unrest in Rome. Four men have been acclaimed emperor, only to be assassinated. Now Vespasian, the very general besieging Jerusalem, has been crowned. What does this mean for the war? Things are uncertain. The price of oil is skyrocketing—olive oil, that is. The world is in turmoil. Where do you look for the future?

Your village population is mixed, Jews and Gentiles, and tensions are high. Neighbors fear one another. Families fracture along ethnic lines. One small sect refuses to fight on either side, followers of a Galilean rabbi named Jesus, who was crucified for insurrection about forty years ago. Roman loyalists suspect them of continuing the alleged insurrection of their founder. The rabbis call them heretics, and the Zealot rebels dismiss their founder as ineffective against Roman oppression. But you are intrigued by their claim that Jesus' crucifixion is a symbol of God's "good news" for Israel and Rome. You ask, if this Jesus really was God's prophet, how is his execution good news for us? Someone hands you a scroll with a title scribbled on it, "The Beginning of the Good News about Jesus, the Messiah, the Son of God."

The title is provocative. The "good news" is foremost a story about Jesus. The word "messiah" reflects Jewish apocalyptic traditions about the eschatological inbreaking of God, who shakes the world, turning it right side up to restore the proper order under God's reign. The designation "Son of God" challenges the claim of *divi filius* found on many Roman coins next to portraits of emperors. So we might expect this story to challenge the established political order and side with Israel against pagan oppressors. But the story opens with John the Baptist preaching repentance. How does this make sense of the present political turmoil?

To help his readers understand their troubled situation, Mark proclaims the good news of Jesus. But to understand Jesus, he looks back to the Scriptures of Israel. Mark's good news begins not with a birth story of Jesus (as in Matthew), not with the birth story of John the Baptist (as in Luke), and not with the beginning of time (as in John). Rather, the good news of the Gospel of Mark begins with a hearkening back to the words of the prophets. Indeed, we cannot understand Christian faith adequately without understanding the Jewish roots of that faith. Whatever we think God is doing in our world today, and whatever we think God did in Jesus Christ, should be consistent with what God was doing all along in Israel.

Mark says the beginning of the gospel is "just as" Isaiah said. It is not that Isaiah was predicting John the Baptist, but Mark sees an analogy between Isaiah's "voice in the wilderness" and the preaching of John "in the wilderness." Isaiah provides a frame of reference for understanding the Baptist. In its own context, Isaiah looks for God's intervention to restore Israel from

Babylonian exile. For Mark, John is like the voice that announces "comfort" to the exiles in Babylon. Although first-century Jews were not in exile, they were under foreign occupation. It was as if the Babylonian exile had followed them home,[1] and Isaiah 40 offered a fitting analogy for those who looked for restoration.

But lest his readers get the wrong idea of a triumphalist stance toward Rome, Mark also alludes to the prophet Malachi's words, "See, I am sending my messenger to prepare the way before me" (Mal. 3:1). That oracle also looks forward to God's intervention, but not for restoration. In Malachi, God's messenger clears the way by calling God's people to repentance. Just as Malachi warned of God's judgment against the sins of Israel, so John preached repentance for the forgiveness of sins. Mark's juxtaposition with Malachi helps us to notice that there is also a reprimand in the comforting oracle of Isaiah (40:27). We who look to God to deliver us from our enemies must first examine ourselves to see whether we are fit to stand before a righteous God.

Scripture proclaims hope for troubled souls and judgment for the self-assured. Against our human tendency to read the Bible in self-justifying ways, confirming our prejudices and excusing our resentments, we must learn to read self-critically, allowing Scripture to correct us. As the Swiss Reformed theologian Karl Barth says, "only when the Bible grasps at us," does it become for us the word of God.[2]

Mark teaches us to see God by looking to Jesus. But to understand Jesus correctly, Mark looks way back to the prophets of Israel. He sees them looking forward in anticipation of God's intervention. When he stands with them and looks as they look, he sees John the Baptist in line with them and looking in the same direction. As Mark looks at John looking at Jesus, he sees himself in perspective. And so, with eyes trained by the prophets to look repentantly and trustingly for God, Mark too looks to Jesus. Mark's story invites his readers to see Israel, Rome, and themselves in a different light—to see themselves in the crowds listening to the prophet John, seeking direction for our future. We look for God's definitive intervention to set things right. John points us to Jesus, who came so long ago and who for us is yet coming. As in the past, Jesus may shock us when he comes and shows us who we really are before God. Our only hope is to join with John in confessing our sins and looking to the coming of the Mightier One. Come, Lord Jesus.

1. N. T. Wright, *The New Testament and the People of God* (Minneapolis: Fortress Press, 1992), 268–71.
2. Karl Barth, *Church Dogmatics* I/1, trans. G.W. Bromiley, 2nd ed. (Edinburgh: T. & T. Clark, 1975), 109–10.

PRAYERS OF INTERCESSION

Let us pray to the Lord, saying,
Hear us, O God; your mercy is great.

We come to you this day, O God,
with a deepening anticipation of your birth among us.
We thank you for the gift of your love.
Hear us, O God; **your mercy is great.**

We pray for the church throughout the world,
and for all the ministries that build up the body of Christ,
that in our many vocations we may serve to your glory.
Hear us, O God; **your mercy is great.**

We pray for this nation and for all nations,
remembering especially those who are victims of political
    and social injustice.
We pray for elected officials and all leaders,
that they will govern with courage and equity.
Hear us, O God; **your mercy is great.**

We pray for all in need:
for the sick, the destitute, and the dying;
for strangers in our land, for the invisible ones;
for the elderly and children; for parents and grandparents;
for those who live alone and those who live lonely in the
    midst of family.
Hear us, O God; **your mercy is great.**

We remember with mercy those who sleep without shelter,
cold and vulnerable, lacking enough food;
those who are overworked
and those who have no work.
Stir up in us the capacity to see ourselves in their struggles
and to act so that others may have life abundant.
Hear us, O God; **your mercy is great.**

We pray for this community, for our neighbors and friends,
and for those with whom we study and work.

Guide and strengthen all people in our common life
to know the gifts of your grace and love.
Hear us, O God; **your mercy is great.**

May all that we ask and all that you see is needed in our world,
be given to your people;
through Christ, our Lord. **Amen.**

DISMISSAL
Prepare the way of the Lord;   *Isa. 40:3; Mark 1:3*
make known his wonderful works;
may grace and peace abide with you
on your journey.

Midweek Service: Week Three

Isaiah 11:1–10

¹A shoot shall come out from the stump of Jesse,
and a branch shall grow out of his roots.
²The spirit of the LORD shall rest on him,
the spirit of wisdom and understanding,
the spirit of counsel and might,
the spirit of knowledge and the fear of the LORD.
³His delight shall be in the fear of the LORD.

He shall not judge by what his eyes see,
or decide by what his ears hear;
⁴but with righteousness he shall judge the poor,
and decide with equity for the meek of the earth;
he shall strike the earth with the rod of his mouth,
and with the breath of his lips he shall kill the wicked.
⁵Righteousness shall be the belt around his waist,
and faithfulness the belt around his loins.

⁶The wolf shall live with the lamb,
the leopard shall lie down with the kid,
the calf and the lion and the fatling together,
and a little child shall lead them.
⁷The cow and the bear shall graze,
their young shall lie down together;
and the lion shall eat straw like the ox.
⁸The nursing child shall play over the hole of the asp,
and the weaned child shall put its hand on the adder's den.
⁹They will not hurt or destroy
on all my holy mountain;
for the earth will be full of the knowledge of the LORD
as the waters cover the sea.

¹⁰On that day the root of Jesse shall stand as a signal to the peoples; the
nations shall inquire of him, and his dwelling shall be glorious.

[29]The next day [John] saw Jesus coming toward him and declared, "Here is the Lamb of God who takes away the sin of the world! [30]This is he of whom I said, 'After me comes a man who ranks ahead of me because he was before me.' [31]I myself did not know him; but I came baptizing with water for this reason, that he might be revealed to Israel." [32]And John testified, "I saw the Spirit descending from heaven like a dove, and it remained on him. [33]I myself did not know him, but the one who sent me to baptize with water said to me, 'He on whom you see the Spirit descend and remain is the one who baptizes with the Holy Spirit.' [34]And I myself have seen and have testified that this is the Son of God."

ORDER OF WORSHIP

OPENING WORDS / CALL TO WORSHIP

Behold, the Lamb of God who takes away the sins
of the world. *John 1:29, 33*
**By water and the Holy Spirit, we are cleansed
and empowered
to come before the Lord in praise and thanksgiving.
Blessed be the name of the Lord!**

CALL TO CONFESSION

Let us lay before God and one another
the distances between us,
the impatience, idolatries, and lack of compassion
that form our confessions this day.
For if we say we have no sin, we deceive ourselves.
Yet in mercy, God will forgive us and renew us.

PRAYER OF CONFESSION

**Gracious and welcoming God,
have mercy on your people.
We confess that we do not believe in your incarnation.
We do not heed your word each day in all that we say and do.
We do not see our neighbors, families, and friends
as beloved children whom you have made.
In your mercy, forgive us,**

for we repent of our ways
and look to your power
to heal us and raise us up,
so that, at the last, you will gather us to you
and give us peace. Amen.

DECLARATION OF FORGIVENESS
The reign of God has come near;
the repentant will be judged with righteousness.
You are forgiven.
Be filled with hope,
believing in the power of the risen Christ
to bring you to new life.
Rejoice and believe.

PRAYER OF THE DAY
O Root of Jesse, O Peace, stir up your power
    within us,   *Isa. 11:10*
that in this time we may await with abundant expectation
the fulfillment of your eternal presence in creation,
for you live and reign among us,
Maker, Savior, and Giver of Life,
one God, now and forever. **Amen.**

SCRIPTURE READINGS

HOMILY
Christ has no body now on earth but yours,
    no hands but yours,
    no feet but yours,
Yours are the eyes through which to look out
    Christ's compassion to the world;
Yours are the feet with which he is to go about doing good;
Yours are the hands with which he is to bless men now.

This poem is attributed to Teresa of Avila, a sixteenth-century Spanish mystic, composed by her in a letter sent to her nuns toward the end of her life, although the actual documentation is obscure. Nevertheless, it has taken on a popular presence in Christian spirituality and reflects a common understanding of what some call an incarnational theology—the idea that we are to be Jesus Christ to the world. At its foundation, incarnational theology reminds us all that God became incarnate—became flesh—in Jesus Christ to embody fully God's love for the world. Teresa of Avila takes this incarnational theology one step further and calls on us to incarnate Christ in our own selves and to love the world as Jesus did, even to the point of "always carrying in the body the death of Jesus, so that the life of Jesus may also be made visible in our bodies" as the apostle Paul writes to the church at Corinth (2 Cor. 4:10).

In this text in John, however, we come to see a different understanding of incarnational theology. Here, John the Baptist sees Jesus, God incarnate, coming and calls attention to Jesus, testifying to all within hearing distance that this is one who baptizes with the Holy Spirit. Later, when John is standing with two of his disciples, he sees Jesus walk by and tells his disciples that Jesus is the "Lamb of God!" John's disciples follow Jesus, and Jesus then begins to call his own disciples. Throughout these verses, John the Baptist plays an important role. He provides testimony as to who Jesus is and points the way so that others come to recognize Jesus Christ.

In the 1990s, when the What Would Jesus Do? campaign was all the rage, many people wore bracelets with the letters WWJD on them. For some, it was just a fad, but ideally, the bracelets were tangible reminders that we are followers of Jesus and that we are to be guided by his actions in every facet of our lives. It's a good question to ask, "what would Jesus do?" but it may also mislead us into thinking that we can really know what Jesus would do in a given situation and that, if we did know, we would be capable of doing it.

Teresa of Avila and the apostle Paul make a valuable point, that we are to live lives that embody Christ, but it is equally important that we not take on some messianic identity that says we are Christ to the world. How many of us are guilty of having a messiah complex, filling our schedules and stressing over ordinary things as if the world relied on us in order to keep turning? Friends, I have some good news for you: The Messiah has come! Now here's some even better news: You are not him! The real danger in a distorted incarnational theology is that we come to believe that if we truly are Christ's body in the world, then if the world is going to be saved, we have to do it.

It may be better for us to ask, not so much WWJD? but rather WWJBD? What would John the Baptist do? John knows that he is not the Messiah, the savior on whom everyone has been waiting. John knows that his job is to point to Christ, to spread the news that Jesus is the Son of God.

In addition to declaring Jesus' divine lineage, John the Baptist's testimony includes a declaration of Jesus as "the Lamb of God." While the image of a "lamb" often communicates a weak, vulnerable animal ready for sacrifice or slaughter, as it is used here and in some other Jewish writings, the lamb is powerful. The lamb reigns in the heavens and will bring about judgment on the wicked and secure salvation for the righteous. It is in relation to this lamb that John recognizes his own inferiority or lower rank. Jesus "ranks ahead" of John because Jesus precedes him in time (having been preexistent), because Jesus baptizes with the Spirit and John only with water, and finally because in God's plans John is preparatory in function. Jesus' superior rank and priority mean that any disciples of John, if they rightly digest his testimony, must move their allegiance to Jesus.

As we prepare to welcome the Messiah into the world and into our lives, let us challenge ourselves to be more like John the Baptist—to call attention to Jesus Christ and then to say to all who are within hearing distance, "Hey, look! See! God is alive. God is in our midst. The Holy Spirit is at work in us and through and for us and even in spite of us! Behold! The Lamb of God!"

PRAYERS OF INTERCESSION

[A time of silence follows each petition.]
God of steadfast love,
you raise us up when we fall
and place our feet on steady ground.
Strengthened by your faithfulness,
we offer our prayers
in thanksgiving for the grace that is ours in Christ.

We pray for the mission of your church,
that we may proclaim the good news of the age
as we put our trust in you.

We pray for the world,
that your saving love may reach to the ends of the earth
as we serve the common good.

We pray for all who suffer,
that we may heed their cry
as we share in your steadfast mercy.

We pray for your creation,
that we may safeguard its well-being
as we labor together for redemption.

We remember before you those who have died
and pray for those who will die today,
that they may know your peace.

Through Christ, with Christ, in Christ,
in the unity of the Holy Spirit,
all glory and honor are yours, almighty Father,
forever and ever. **Amen.**

DISMISSAL

Go now into the world with arms stretched wide,
pointing not to ourselves in pride
or toward others in judgment
but to Jesus the Messiah, the Son of God.   *John 1:34*

Midweek Service: Week Four

Isaiah 35:1–10

¹The wilderness and the dry land shall be glad,
  the desert shall rejoice and blossom;
like the crocus ²it shall blossom abundantly,
  and rejoice with joy and singing.
The glory of Lebanon shall be given to it,
  the majesty of Carmel and Sharon.
They shall see the glory of the LORD,
  the majesty of our God.

³Strengthen the weak hands,
  and make firm the feeble knees.
⁴Say to those who are of a fearful heart,
  "Be strong, do not fear!
Here is your God.
  He will come with vengeance,
with terrible recompense.
  He will come and save you."

⁵Then the eyes of the blind shall be opened,
  and the ears of the deaf unstopped;
⁶then the lame shall leap like a deer,
  and the tongue of the speechless sing for joy.
For waters shall break forth in the wilderness,
  and streams in the desert;
⁷the burning sand shall become a pool,
  and the thirsty ground springs of water;
the haunt of jackals shall become a swamp,
  the grass shall become reeds and rushes.

⁸A highway shall be there,
  and it shall be called the Holy Way;
the unclean shall not travel on it,

but it shall be for God's people;
no traveler, not even fools, shall go astray.
⁹No lion shall be there,
nor shall any ravenous beast come up on it;
they shall not be found there,
but the redeemed shall walk there.
¹⁰And the ransomed of the LORD shall return,
and come to Zion with singing;
everlasting joy shall be upon their heads;
they shall obtain joy and gladness,
and sorrow and sighing shall flee away.

Matthew 11:2–11

²When John heard in prison what the Messiah was doing, he sent word by his disciples ³and said to him, "Are you the one who is to come, or are we to wait for another?" ⁴Jesus answered them, "Go and tell John what you hear and see: ⁵the blind receive their sight, the lame walk, the lepers are cleansed, the deaf hear, the dead are raised, and the poor have good news brought to them. ⁶And blessed is anyone who takes no offense at me."

⁷As they went away, Jesus began to speak to the crowds about John: "What did you go out into the wilderness to look at? A reed shaken by the wind? ⁸What then did you go out to see? Someone dressed in soft robes? Look, those who wear soft robes are in royal palaces. ⁹What then did you go out to see? A prophet? Yes, I tell you, and more than a prophet. ¹⁰This is the one about whom it is written,

'See, I am sending my messenger ahead of you,
who will prepare your way before you.'

¹¹Truly I tell you, among those born of women no one has arisen greater than John the Baptist; yet the least in the kingdom of heaven is greater than he."

ORDER OF WORSHIP

OPENING WORDS / CALL TO WORSHIP
Let anyone with ears listen;   *Matt. 11:15, 4–5*
the Lord brings good news!
The blind will see, the lame will walk;
the dead are raised and the poor are blessed.
Praise the name of the Lord!

CALL TO CONFESSION

Let the desert rejoice,   *Isa. 35:1, 4*
and let the dry land be glad,
for God has come to save us.
Let us confess our sin.

PRAYER OF CONFESSION

God of majesty and glory,   *Isa. 35:1–10*
we are thirsty for your grace.
You made a way for us in the wilderness,
and still, in our foolishness, we go astray.
We hide our eyes from your presence.
We do not listen to your word.
We are lifeless when we ought to dance
and speechless when we ought to sing.

Forgive us, O Lord.
Speak peace to our fearful hearts,
strengthen our weak hands,
and make firm our feeble knees
as we seek to follow in your holy way. Amen.

DECLARATION OF FORGIVENESS

Now return to the Lord with joy and gladness.   *Isa. 35:10*
Sing a song of redemption!
Let sorrow and sighing be no more.
In Jesus Christ we are forgiven.
Thanks be to God.

PRAYER OF THE DAY

Holy God, your prophets have long spoken   *Matt. 11:2–11*
of the one who would come to save us.
Now the promise is fulfilled;
now your kingdom has come near.
Send us as messengers of your way,
to go and tell all the world
of the wonders we have seen
and the good news we have heard;
through Jesus Christ our Lord. **Amen.**

HOMILY

The Gospels report that those who encountered Jesus were regularly confused about who he really was. Jesus himself eventually asked his disciples, "Who do people say that I am?" (Matt. 16:13). Those whose existence is bound up with that of Jesus' end up posing the same question about themselves: Who am I really? Such questions of identity come to the fore in today's Gospel reading, in which John wonders who Jesus really is, and Jesus notes that the crowd wonders who John really is. Jesus alone can bring clarity to both questions.

John is now in prison, a stark reminder of how his prophetic witness has been received, and sends his disciples to ask Jesus if he is truly the one promised to Israel. The question brings us up short, since John had clearly witnessed to Jesus as the Messiah at the time of Jesus' baptism. In Matthew's narrative, John seems to raise his question because of his own imprisonment under Herod, but something else has profoundly changed in the meantime. John is now no longer the predecessor and preparer, no longer the messenger who goes before Christ's face. Rather, the one who now testifies to Christ is no less than Christ himself. Christ himself prepares the witness that John must receive. John must hear for himself that in Christ the blind see, the lame walk, lepers are cleansed, the deaf hear, the dead are raised up, and the poor have good news preached to them. He must become a disciple, and so, he seeks clarity on the true identity of the one he follows, the one with whom he is less acquainted in reality than he was in prophecy.

The question would seem to be a simple one, "Are you the one who is to come, or are we to wait for another?" As is so often the case, Jesus responds to John's question indirectly. More to the point, Jesus' response enlarges the scope of the question, with echoes from the prophet Isaiah that provide glimpses of a new age in which the wounds of Israel will be healed. Matthew parallel's Isaiah in saying that, with the advent of Jesus, the blind see (Matt. 9:27–31 and Isa. 29:18; 35:5); the lame walk (Matt. 9:2–8 and Isa. 35:6); the deaf hear (Matt. 9:32–34 and Isa. 35:5); the dead are raised (Matt. 9:18–19, 23–26 and Isa. 26:19); and the poor are cared for (Matt. 9:35–38 and Isa. 29:19; 42:7; 61:1–2).

Perhaps the most intriguing member of the list is the final entry, "the poor have good news brought to them." The poor (*ptōchoi*) refers to the destitute, the down and out, the desperate. It is interesting that Jesus culminates his response to John with a reference to the poor. The poor are always the test case of the covenant. If the Torah's communal covenant is kept, then the promises of Deuteronomy 15 will come to pass. The reference to the poor as a group, rather than as people with individual needs, suggests a systemic concern for the injustice and oppression visited on the poor by the rulers, whether Caesar, Herod Antipas in Galilee, or the high-priestly families in Jerusalem.

It is in this context that we can understand the beatitude with which Jesus concludes his remarks, "blessed is anyone who takes no offense at me." The issue is pointed. Jesus is not talking about an amiable disagreement in a policy debate by saying, blessed are the analysts and courtiers. John and Jesus share one crucial characteristic: they are both willing to risk entering the public arena against well-prepared opponents, even when it means speaking truth to those in power, a very dangerous occupation that can land the prophet in prison or on a cross. All this speaks about how the old age continues to operate. Those in power stay in power. The powerful exploit the powerless. It is a vicious cycle that only an advent can change. Both John and Jesus are part of that advent as it struggles to come to life.

The crowds that had gone into the wilderness to behold John had not really understood that John's identity was wrapped up with that of Jesus. So, Jesus asks them what they had expected to find. A reed shaken by the wind, like an emaciated holy man? A man dressed in fine, soft robes, like a king? Or a prophet? Jesus declares that John is indeed a prophet (a new Elijah, he will later say in verse 14), yet even "prophet" does not adequately describe John. As one preparing the way for Christ, John has surpassed the great prophets. In the whole history of Israel, he has no equal. Among those born of woman, truly no one rises above him. Nevertheless, as one who must still learn to become a disciple, John is least of those in the kingdom of heaven. John who had preceded Jesus must now learn to follow him; the one who prepared the way for Jesus must now receive him. The first will be last, and the last will be first.

John is both the culmination of prophecy and its conclusion, for he is a bridge between this age and the age to come. In describing John with such a paradox, Jesus seems to be saying that "just when you think you have measured the magnitude of this advent of heaven's reign, you discover that you have not even begun to capture it." As the reign of heaven comes into focus, John suddenly diminishes in importance; yet, even though he is least, he still belongs. He has a role to play in this kingdom, as do all who follow Christ, announcing Jesus' reign over all earthly kingdoms and participating in the Messiah's work of justice and healing for an aching world.

PRAYERS OF INTERCESSION

Lord God, in this dry and dusty place, *Isa. 35:1–10*
pour out the power of your Spirit on all those in need.
Strengthen the weak hands
and make firm the feeble knees
Comfort those who live in fear,
"Be strong, your God is here."
Open the eyes of the blind
that we all may see your glory.
Unstop the ears of the deaf and free the muted tongues
that we all may sing your song.
For all those who hunger and thirst
Lord, let your river flow.
Let all generations see your blessing,
for your name is holy and your mercy is great.
Then we will sing out with joy and glorify you forever;
through Jesus Christ our Savior. Amen.

DISMISSAL

Be strong and bold; do not fear! *Isa. 35:4, Matt. 11:4*
Tell the world what you see and hear.

❧ ADDITIONAL RESOURCES ❧

Service of Hope and Healing

The twinkling lights and merry songs of Christmas can, in cruel contrast, deepen the darkness and gloom felt by those struggling with grief, depression, or illness. For this reason, many churches offer a special time of worship during the Advent season to offer comfort, healing, and hope. Sometimes called a "Longest Night" service, the service is held close to Christmas, when the winter solstice of December 21 makes the days shorter and darker than at any other time in the year.

The service suggested here features readings from the book of Psalms that give voice to our feelings of pain, loss, and the hope we cling to in the midst of despair. Readers should allow several minutes for contemplation after each psalm. A homily may be included, or time for laying on of hands, if you so choose. Somber Advent hymns and soft candlelight will give a sense of abiding faith and the persistent light of Christ in the darkest areas of our lives.

ORDER OF WORSHIP

OPENING WORDS / CALL TO WORSHIP
We cry to the Lord who counts and collects our tears.   *Ps. 56:8*
Be with us now.
In our grief and our pain, our bodies and spirits cry out.
Hear us, O Lord. Amen.

HYMN

PRAYER

The days are short. The nights are long. Lord, your universe mirrors the reality of our hearts, revealing your gracious spirit that mourns with us in grief, cries with us in sorrow, sits with us in despair. You are not a distant God, removed from human pain, but a faithful companion closer to us than our tears. Help us to feel your presence now as we remember and reflect, seeking your healing touch and the hope that was promised and delivered in Jesus Christ your Son. Amen.

LIGHTING OF THE ADVENT CANDLES

[Reader 1]: We light these candles in thanksgiving for loved ones lost, for past health and joy that now seems distant.

[Reader 2]: We light these candles in prayer, that we will feel God's love in our present sorrow.

[Reader 3]: We light these candles in hope, for the promises of God yet to be revealed.

[All]: **Glory to God. Amen.**

HYMN

SCRIPTURE READINGS

Psalm 13

¹How long, O Lord? Will you forget me forever?
　　How long will you hide your face from me?
²How long must I bear pain in my soul,
　　and have sorrow in my heart all day long?
How long shall my enemy be exalted over me?

³Consider and answer me, O Lord my God!
　　Give light to my eyes, or I will sleep the sleep of death,
⁴and my enemy will say, "I have prevailed";
　　my foes will rejoice because I am shaken.

⁵But I trusted in your steadfast love;
　　my heart shall rejoice in your salvation.
⁶I will sing to the Lord,
because he has dealt bountifully with me.
[Silence for contemplation]

Psalms 61:1–4; 62:1–2

[61:1]Hear my cry, O God;
     listen to my prayer.
[2]From the end of the earth I call to you,
     when my heart is faint.

Lead me to the rock
     that is higher than I;
[3]for you are my refuge,
     a strong tower against the enemy.

[4]Let me abide in your tent forever,
     find refuge under the shelter of your wings.   *Selah*

[62:1]For God alone my soul waits in silence;
     from him comes my salvation.
[2]He alone is my rock and my salvation,
     my fortress; I shall never be shaken.
     [Silence for contemplation]

Psalm 139:7–12

[7]Where can I go from your spirit?
     Or where can I flee from your presence?
[8]If I ascend to heaven, you are there;
     if I make my bed in Sheol, you are there.
[9]If I take the wings of the morning
     and settle at the farthest limits of the sea,
[10]even there your hand shall lead me,
     and your right hand shall hold me fast.
[11]If I say, "Surely the darkness shall cover me,
     and the light around me become night,"
[12]even the darkness is not dark to you;
     the night is as bright as the day,
     for darkness is as light to you.
     [Silence for contemplation]

Psalm 23

¹The L{ORD} is my shepherd, I shall not want.
　　²He makes me lie down in green pastures; he leads me
　　　　beside still waters;
　　³he restores my soul.
　He leads me in right paths
　　　for his name's sake.

　　⁴Even though I walk through the darkest valley,
　　　I fear no evil;
　for you are with me;
　　　your rod and your staff—
　　　they comfort me.

　　⁵You prepare a table before me
　　　in the presence of my enemies;
　you anoint my head with oil;
　　　my cup overflows.
⁶Surely goodness and mercy shall follow me
　　　all the days of my life,
　and I shall dwell in the house of the L{ORD}
　　　my whole life long.
　　[Silence for contemplation]

HOMILY (OPTIONAL)

THE LORD'S SUPPER (OPTIONAL)

HYMN

CHARGE AND BLESSING

May Jesus, the life—the life that is light for all people—
　　shine in your heart.　　　　　　　　　　　　　*John 1:4–5*
No matter how small, no matter how dim, that light
　　will stubbornly shine.
And the darkness will not overcome it.
Go in peace, with courage to face the coming days
　　with hope, with God by your side. Amen.

SONG SUGGESTIONS

"Come, Thou Long-Expected Jesus" (*CH* 125, *EH* 66, *ELW* 254, *GC* 323, *GTG* 82–83, *TNCH* 122, *UMH* 196)

"Comfort, Comfort Now My People" (*CH* 122–123, *EH* 67, *ELW* 256, *GC* 326, *GTG* 87, *TNCH* 101)

"For You, O Lord, My Soul in Stillness Waits" (*GC* 328, *GTG* 89)

"O Come, O Come, Emmanuel" (*CH* 119, *ELW* 257, *GC* 317, *GTG* 88, *TNCH* 116, *UMH* 211)

"O Day of God, Draw Nigh" (*TNCH* 611, *UMH* 730)

"The People Who Walked in Darkness" (*GTG* 86)

"While We Are Waiting, Come" (*GTG* 92)

Eucharistic Prayers for Advent and Christmas

Option 1

The Lord be with you.
And also with you.
Lift up your hearts.
We lift them to the Lord.
Let us give thanks to the Lord our God.
It is right to give our thanks and praise.

How can we thank you, O God?
For sun and moon and stars,
for breath and life and all things good,
for your steadfast promise and your faithful love,
for the day that is surely coming
when all things will be made new.

With saints, with angels, and with the whole creation,
we join the ancient and eternal hymn:

**Holy, holy, holy Lord, God of power and might,
heaven and earth are full of your glory.
Hosanna in the highest.
Blessed is he who comes in the name of the Lord.
Hosanna in the highest.**

We give you thanks, Holy God, for Jesus,
who came to be your living Word,
to baptize us with Spirit and fire,

to feed the hungry, to humble the mighty,
and to announce the good news of your coming realm.
With thanksgiving, we remember how, when the hour had come,
Jesus took his place at the table with the apostles.

He said to them, I will not eat this Passover again
until it is fulfilled in the kingdom of God.

Then Jesus took bread,
and when he had given thanks,
he broke it and gave it to them, saying,
This is my body, which is given for you.
Do this in remembrance of me.

After supper, he took a cup, saying,
This cup that is poured out for you
is the new covenant in my blood.
I will not drink of the fruit of the vine
until the kingdom of God comes.

With thanks and praise we offer ourselves to you,
sharing this holy meal,
remembering Christ's dying and rising,
and praying: Come Lord Jesus!

Christ has died,
Christ is risen,
Christ will come again.

Pour out your Holy Spirit upon us—
this bread, this cup, these people—
Christ's body and blood,
given in love for the world.
Make us one in the Spirit,
one in the church,
and one with Christ our Lord.

Make us gentle, joyful, thankful people,
serving our neighbors, worshiping you alone.

Keep us in the peace of Christ
until you gather us at your table in glory.
Even now, a voice is crying in the wilderness:
prepare the way of the Lord!

Through Christ, with Christ, in Christ,
in the unity of the Holy Spirit,
all glory and honor are yours, almighty God,
now and forever. **Amen.**

Option 2

The Lord be with you.
And with your Spirit.
Lift up your hearts.
We lift them to the Lord.
Let us give thanks to the Lord our God.
It is right to give our thanks and praise.

It is right and a good and joyful thing
always and everywhere to give thanks to you,
Almighty God, creator of heaven and earth.
You call all people to follow your paths of justice and peace,
beating their swords into plowshares
and their spears into pruning hooks.
In the light of your holy Word we look for the day
when nation shall not lift up sword against nation,
or learn war anymore.   *Isa. 2:4*
Therefore, with the entire company of heaven,
and with your people on earth who live in this hope,
we praise you and join in the never-ending hymn:

Holy, holy, holy Lord, God of power and might,
heaven and earth are full of your glory.
Hosanna in the highest.
Blessed is he who comes in the name of the Lord.
Hosanna in the highest.

Holy are you and blessed is Jesus Christ your Son,
for he is Immanuel, God with us.
Fulfilling the expectations of the prophets
he healed the blind and the lame,
cleansed the lepers, opened the ears of the deaf,
raised the dead, and brought good news to the poor.   *Matt. 11:5*
Through his life, death, and resurrection
you manifest your new covenant with humankind,
and through the church of his disciples
you give testimony to the power of your salvation
    for the world.

For on the night he was betrayed he took bread,
gave thanks to you, broke the bread, and gave it to his disciples, saying,
Take, eat, this is my body given for you. Do this in remembrance of me.
When the supper was over, he took the cup and gave thanks, saying,
Drink this, all of you.
This is my blood of the new covenant
poured out for many for the forgiveness of sins.
Do this is remembrance of me.

Therefore in remembrance of all your mighty acts in Jesus Christ,
we give ourselves in praise and thanksgiving as a living sacrifice
in union with Christ's offering for the world as we declare:
Christ has died,
Christ is risen,
Christ will come again.

Send your Holy Spirit upon us, gathered here out of love for you,
and on these gifts of bread and wine.
Let the bread we break
be a true fellowship in the body of Christ.
Let the cup we share
be a true participation in the new covenant in his blood.
By your Spirit empower us to be Christ for the world,
serving in his name
until the earth shall be full of the knowledge of the Lord
as the waters cover the sea.   *Isa. 11:9b*
Through your son Jesus Christ,
with the Holy Spirit in your holy church,
all glory and honor is yours, almighty God,
now and forever. **Amen.**

CHRISTMAS DAY

Option 1

The Lord be with you.
And also with you.
Lift up your hearts.
We lift them to the Lord.
Let us give our thanks to the Lord our God.
It is right to give our thanks and praise.

It is good to give you thanks,
O God, source of abundant life;
through Jesus Christ your eternal Word
who creates all things
by the working of your Spirit.

For he is the reflection of your glory,   *Heb. 1:3*
the very imprint of your being.
In him you have become one with us
that we might become one with you.

And so we raise our voices with saints and angels
and all creation in joyful praise to you singing,

Holy, holy, holy Lord, God of goodness and life,
heaven and earth are full of your glory.
Hosanna in the highest.
Blessed is the one who comes in the name of the Lord.
Hosanna in the highest.

Holy and wondrous God, *Heb. 1:1–2*
long ago you spoke to our ancestors
in many and various ways.
And in these last days you have spoken to us
in your Word made flesh, Jesus,
who proclaimed your dream of peace.

He gave himself for our weary world,
accepting death so that we might live,
and held our darkness deep within
until through cross and grave and empty tomb
he set us free for love.

On the night before he died for us
our Lord Jesus Christ took bread,
and when he had given thanks to you,
he broke it, and gave it to his disciples, and said,

Take, eat. This is my body, which is given for you.
Do this for the remembrance of me.
After supper he took the cup of wine;
and when he had given thanks,
he gave it to them and said,
Drink this all of you.
This is my blood poured out for you and for all
for the forgiveness of sins.
Whenever you drink it,
do this for the remembrance of me.

And so we proclaim the mystery of faith:
Christ has died,
Christ is risen,
Christ will come again.

Recalling his death and resurrection,
and longing for his coming in glory
we offer you these gifts of bread and wine,
and our lives in thanks and praise.
Pour out your Spirit upon these gifts that they may be for us
the body and blood of our Savior Jesus Christ.

Pour out your Spirit upon us that we might be
a people of grace and truth,
bearing good news of joy in every season.

And bring us at the last with [Mary and Joseph, and] all your saints
to that vision of eternal splendor for which you have created us.
Through Jesus Christ our Lord,
by him, with him, and in him,
in the unity of the Holy Spirit,
we worship you, O God,
in songs of everlasting praise. **Amen.**

The Lord be with you.
And also with you.
Lift up your hearts.
We lift them to the Lord.
Let us give thanks to the Lord, our God.
It is right to give our thanks and praise.

In every time and in every place,
it is right that we should give you thanks and honor,
for you shelter your people from age to age.
You came to us as a brother and a friend,
in a likeness we could recognize as one of our own,
showing us the face of the Most High God.

Through the centuries, your witnesses have taught and proclaimed your Word,
giving shape to the truth that your promises are sure
and your presence everlasting.

In communion with all the saints, with angels and shepherds,
we praise your name and join their unending hymn:

Holy, holy, holy Lord, God of power and might,
heaven and earth are full of your glory.
Hosanna in the highest.
Blessed is the one who comes in the name of the Lord.
Hosanna in the highest.

Holy God,
author of time,
one among us,
breath of our bodies,
you are as close to us as skin
and infinite as stars.

You came to us as Jesus of Nazareth,
carpenter and rabbi,
who on the night he was betrayed,

took bread, and gave thanks;
broke it, and gave it to his disciples, saying,
Take and eat; this is my body, given for you.
Do this for the remembrance of me.

Again, after supper, he took the cup, gave thanks,
and gave it for all to drink, saying,
This cup is the new covenant in my blood,
shed for you and for all people for the forgiveness of sin.
Do this for the remembrance of me.

Whenever we eat this bread and drink this cup,
we proclaim today the Lord's blessing,
present in our time just as in ages past,
building the communion of saints even from our own bodies.

Bless us with your presence,
and give us here a foretaste of the feast to come.
Let your Holy Spirit infuse our hearts and minds with joy
so that we may live to praise you, O God,
holy Trinity, now and forever. **Amen.**

Acknowledgments

Some materials in this volume were drawn from *Feasting on the Word: Preaching the Revised Common Lectionary*, edited by David L. Bartlett and Barbara Brown Taylor, and *Feasting on the Word Worship Companion*, edited by Kimberly Bracken Long.

Prayers and liturgical material were written by Kimberly Clayton, David Gambrell, Daniel Geslin, Kimberly Bracken Long, L. Edward Phillips, Melinda Quivik, and Carol L. Wade, with Jennifer Carlier, Marissa Galvan-Valle, Kathryn Schneider Halliburton, L'Anni Hill, Jessica Miller Kelley, Elizabeth C. Knowlton, Franklin Lewis, Elizabeth H. Shannon, and Margaret LaMotte Torrence.

Children's sermons were written by Jessica Miller Kelley and Carol Wehrheim.

Homilies were drawn from essays by the following:
Midweek Service 1: Lillian Daniel, Judy Yates Siker, Stephen A. Cooper, and George Stroup
Midweek Service 2: Christopher Hutson and Judy Yates Siker
Midweek Service 3: Rodger Y. Nishioka and Troy A. Miller
Midweek Service 4: John P. Burgess and William R. Herzog II

Scripture Index